THE GREAT PALACE
OF THE MOSCOW
KREMLIN

THE GREAT PALACE OF THE MOSCOW KREMLIN

Aurora Art Publishers • Leningrad

Compiled and introduced by
G. MARKOVA

Translated from the Russian by
M. WILKINSON

Layout and design by
A. YULIKOV

Photography by
A. ALEXANDROV and
E. STEINERT

© Aurora Art Publishers, Leningrad, 1981, 1990
Printed and bound in Yugoslavia

Б $\dfrac{4902020000\text{-}861}{023(01)\text{-}90}$ 1-90

ISBN 5-7300-0284-X

The Great Palace, a majestic, light-coloured building which stands atop Borovitsky Hill in the Kremlin, is famous not only in the Soviet Union, but also far beyond its boundaries. It is the seat of the Supreme Soviet of the USSR, the highest legislative body of the Soviet state, and of the Supreme Soviet of the RSFSR, the largest of the Soviet republics. Both chambers of the Soviet Parliament—the Council of the Union and the Council of the Nationalities—meet for combined sessions in the spacious Conference Hall on the second floor, while other rooms and halls of the palace are reserved for the permanent committees of the Supreme Soviet and the Praesidium, advisers, and members of the Secretariat. The Faceted Palace is used for meetings of the Council of Elders. It is in the Great Palace that talks between leaders of the Communist Party and the Soviet Government and foreign delegations take place, and large state and diplomatic receptions and meetings of party and government officials with eminent scientists, scholars, artists, and the foremost workers are held. Up until 1970, foreign ambassadors presented their credentials to the Chairman of the Praesidium of the Supreme Soviet in the St Catherine Hall; in the State and Private Apartments awards are presented to citizens who distinguished themselves in their work, and the committee which chooses the candidates for the International Lenin Peace Prize holds its meetings. The 2nd, 3rd and 4th congresses of the Communist International took place in the palace, and also numerous CPSU congresses; on 7th October, 1978, the third Soviet constitution, was adopted there.

The Conference Hall of the Supreme Soviet was designed and built between 1932 and 1934 by I. Ivanov-Schitz, who joined together the St Andrew and St Alexander Halls, named after the old Russian Orders of Sts Andrew the First-Called and Alexander Nevsky. During reconstruction, the existing brick vaults and their supporting columns were torn down and replaced by one concrete vault, and the new, larger hall was thoroughly reequipped and redecorated in a simple, austere fashion, more suitable for the hall's function than the earlier gaudy decor. As well as the sessions of the Supreme Soviets of the USSR and RSFSR, all-union conferences of workers from various sectors of the economy and congresses of writers, artists, architects, film-makers and actors also take place in the Conference Hall.

The hall covers an area of more than 1,600 square metres with seating for more than 2,500 people. The seats on the main floor, of which there are more than 1,500, are reserved for deputies of the Supreme Soviets of the

USSR and RSFSR, delegates of conferences and congresses and foreign guests. At the front of the hall there is a speaker's dais and, behind it, the chairman's desk. During combined sessions of both chambers of the Supreme Soviet the chairmen of the Councils of the Union and the Nationalities take the chair alternately. Behind the chairman's desk there are seats for the honorary members of the Praesidium; to the right and left of them are rows of seats reserved for the Praesidia of the Supreme Soviet and Council of Ministers. Along the north wall at first-floor level are seven boxes for diplomats and, at the back, a large balcony with seating for about 1,000 visitors. The seats in front of the balcony are set aside for the press. The furniture in the hall, dark walnut upholstered in green leather, is comfortable and functional. The hall was modernized during the 1940s and 50s, when the sound system and simultaneous translation equipment were renovated, and air conditioning was installed. The next general overhaul was in 1968, when the ventilation system was replaced and the lighting and sound systems improved. At the same time, some of the supports were reinforced, the floor of the main section was relaid over steel girders and the number of diplomatic seats was increased.

The Great Kremlin Palace is associated with the name of Lenin: here he met with leaders of Communist and workers' parties and talked with delegates. He made numerous powerful speeches in the St Andrew Hall and took part in the work of the Comintern committees in the former State Bedchamber and St Catherine Hall.

Various rooms of the palace contain works of art devoted to Lenin. In 1939, a marble statue by Sergei Merkurov, one of the veteran Soviet sculptors was erected behind the seats occupied by the Praesidium of the Supreme Soviet in the Conference Hall. This statue, full of inner dynamism, recreates with great force the image of the founder of the Soviet state and party.

In the palace anteroom hangs the large canvas *Lenin Addressing the Third Congress of the Komsomol,* painted in 1950 by a group of artists under the direction of the eminent Soviet master Boris Ioganson. This multifigure work was done to mark the thirtieth anniversary of the Third Congress of the Komsomol, when Lenin called upon Soviet youth to "learn Communism". In this picture we see a spacious hall, packed full of delegates—workers, peasants and soldiers. They sit and stand even on the stage, they crowd into the wings, they press against the dais, wishing to be near Lenin and catch his every word. Calmly and simply, he explains to these young people the tasks which will face them after the victory of the revolution. It is October, 1920, and the Soviet state is under enemy siege. There are shortages of food and fuel in Moscow: it is so cold in the hall that many are wearing overcoats.

Despite these hardships, Lenin's words fill the delegates with confidence in a bright future, to realize which they must study, acquire a complete knowledge of national and world culture and work for peace.

The Great Palace is comprised of an extensive complex of chambers and apartments which has evolved over many centuries. The modern title of *Great Kremlin Palace* has been used since approximately the middle of the

last century to denote the palace built in 1848 by the architect Konstantin
Thon for Emperor Nicholas I. Thon integrated the new building with existing
structures from previous centuries: the Faceted Palace, the Tsarina's Golden
Chamber, and also the Terem Palace together with its churches, which
had formed part of the Great Sovereign's Palace of the fifteenth to
seventeenth centuries.

Borovitsky Hill was the traditional site of royal and princely residences in
the Kremlin. It was there, on the territory now occupied by the west wing of
the palace, that the residence of Prince Ivan Kalita once stood. This was a
wooden building, next to which stood the stone Church of Our Saviour,
erected in 1330.

The ancient chronicles provide us with scarcely more information about the
palace of Prince Dmitry Donskoi, built in the second half of the fourteenth
century: the only structures recorded are a "gold-topped terem", a "throne
room" and "riverside chambers". Even this simple list, however, is of help in
establishing the site of this palace and the orientation of its façades, one of
which extended along the crest of the hill, facing the Moscow River, hence
the name "riverside chambers".

The years 1475–1500, when construction was going on in the Kremlin on an
extremely large scale, were particularly important in shaping the Great
Palace complex. By order of Ivan III, Grand Prince of Moscow, new
walls and fortified towers, which have basically survived to this day, were
erected, the Kremlin cathedrals were built anew and many stone chambers
were constructed.

At that time, a residence within the Kremlin which was grand enough to
reflect the growing importance of Moscow as the head of the Russian state
had become vital to Ivan III for several reasons: the prestige of the capital
city; its extensive international connections; the presence of foreign ambassadors; and even court ceremonial itself, which had become particularly lavish
after his marriage to the Byzantine princess Zoë (Sophia) Palaeologus.

Ivan III's palace was a large, ambitious project and took twenty-one years to
build (1487–1508); its main architects were the Italians Marco Ruffo, Pietro
Antonio Solari and Aloisio da Carcano. Of this edifice, the Faceted Palace,
and the basements on which the Terem Palace was built in the first half
of the seventeenth century, have survived to this day. A major fire which
took place in 1493 held up work for nearly six years, and it was resumed
only in the spring of 1499. Then, according to the annals, "chambers of
stone and brick, with store-rooms and ice-cellars beneath were laid for
Ivan III in the old courtyard near the Cathedral of the Annunciation".
The prince did not live to see the building finished, and it was his son,
Vasily III, who moved into the palace in the spring of 1508.

Of the numerous palace structures erected during the reigns of Ivan III and
Vasily III the following are known from surviving documents and plans: the
riverside chambers (the three chambers, each with its own entrance-hall and
each facing the Moscow River, extended from the Cathedral of the Annunciation in the direction of the Borovitsky Gate); the bedchambers of the

prince and princess (which formed the northern limit of the inner courtyard, behind the ancient Church of the Redeemer in the Wood); and the Faceted Palace, the Refectory and the Middle Golden Chamber, which all opened on to Cathedral Square.

In the second half of the sixteenth century and throughout the seventeenth, Ivan the Terrible, Boris Godunov and the first tsars of the Romanov line remodelled the palace and completed its construction. Tumble-down old buildings were demolished and replaced with new ones on the same site.

These new structures were incorporated into the overall complex of the palace and linked with it by special passageways, terraces, stairs, landings, and connecting galleries. As the palace grew in size it became a conglomeration of state rooms, living quarters and churches, each with a different purpose and design, all arranged upon a tall stone basement, with many rooms intended for household use, most frequently store-rooms and ice-cellars. In places, this basement was intersected by pathways between courtyards. One notable part of the extensive building programme carried out in the Kremlin throughout the seventeenth century was the erection of the Terem Palace for Tsar Mikhail Romanov in the years 1635 and 1636. Also during this time many house-chapels were put up, the living quarters of the royal family were enlarged and remodelled and many indoor and "hanging" gardens were laid out on the upper levels.

The architectural complex of the Great Sovereign's Palace was completed in approximately the second half of the seventeenth century; the building continued, however, throughout the eighteenth and into the first half of the nineteenth century. During the years 1749–53, Francesco Bartolommeo Rastrelli, the celebrated court architect to Empress Elizabeth I, erected a "new stone Winter Palace in the Kremlin" on the site of several old structures which had been demolished. In plan the palace was L-shaped, with its long façade overlooking Cathedral Square and its short façade opening on to the Moscow River. The central part of the shorter façade was surmounted by a Baroque pediment, with figures on the sides of a cartouche showing the imperial crest. Rastrelli's palace survived until 1838, when it was torn down to make room for the Great Kremlin Palace designed by Konstantin Thon.

A grandiose project for Catherine II's Kremlin Palace was worked out between 1767 and 1775 by the famous Russian architect Vasily Bazhenov and his assistant, Mikhail Kazakov, another eminent Russian neo-classical architect. The palace was to have been situated on the slope of the Kremlin hill. The south wall of the Kremlin would have had to be demolished to make way for the spacious terraces, stairways and ramps which were to connect the palace and the river-bank. A magnificent four-storey building 630 metres long was to have been raised on the bank of the Moscow River, with two wings (the west wing to house the Ministries and the east wing, the Theatre) extending outwards into the Kremlin and enclosing its ancient squares and monuments. (There is a model of the palace done on a scale of 1:40 in the Shchusev Museum of Architecture and Architectural Research, Moscow.)

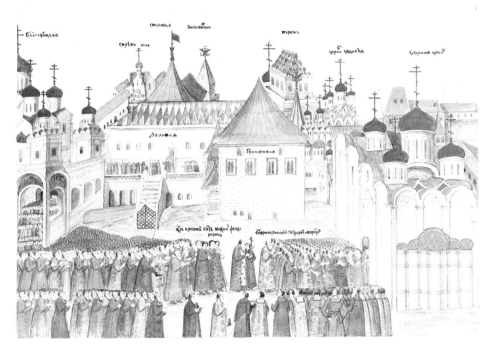

1. *View of the Faceted Palace and the Great Sovereign's Palace from Cathedral Square. 1856 Lithograph from a 1672 drawing in the* Book of the Election and Crowning of Great Sovereign, Tsar and Grand Prince Mikhail Fiodorovich.

The foundation stone of the palace was laid in 1773, but due to the unfavourable political situation and difficulties in obtaining materials, the Russian government had to abandon the project in 1775. It was never completed; Rastrelli's old palace was renovated and, along with the ancient chambers and towers, survived into the nineteenth century. The first years of that century were hard ones for Russia. In 1812 Napoleon's soldiers inflicted significant damage on the palace: burned, looted and partially destroyed, it was a sorry sight.

Extensive renovation work was begun in 1836 under the supervision of Fiodor Richter, a professor of architecture and a member of the Russian Academy of Arts. The old structures, however, were decrepit and unsuitable for an imperial residence. New concepts of beauty and comfort as well as the ruling dynasty's desire to stress the age-old continuity of their power, all this made it necessary to endow the Kremlin residence with great splendour. Nicholas I, therefore, decided to build a new palace. The project was designed and later carried out by Konstantin Thon (1794–1881), a graduate of the St Petersburg Academy of Arts and a pupil of the prominent Russian neo-classical architect Andrei Voronikhin. Thon was already known at court for his ability to construct "extremely sturdy buildings in a short time". In the 1820s he partially reconstructed the Academy of Arts, and in 1837 he planned the embankment along the Neva and put up in front of the Academy of Arts the granite sculptures of ancient Egyptian sphinxes.

9

A follower of Neo-Classicism, Thon also constantly strove to create a new trend in Russian architecture. This is evidenced by his projects for churches with five onion domes in Moscow and St Petersburg and by his book of patterns and designs for erecting churches "in the national spirit", published in 1838. His aesthetic ideas are most vividly reflected in such monumental buildings as the Church of Our Saviour and the Great Kremlin Palace in Moscow.

Other Moscow architects who worked with Thon on the Great Kremlin Palace were F. Richter, N. Chichagov, V. Bakarev, and P. Gerasimov. They were set the task of uniting all the fifteenth- to seventeenth-century buildings in the Kremlin with a new palace, and this consideration was a major factor in determining the final design. The most suitable plan was deemed to be several blocks arranged rectangularly around an inner courtyard. The new palace was raised on the hill with its main façade overlooking the bank of the Moscow River. The Terem Palace formed the north side of the rectangle, the ancient Tsarina's Golden Chamber and Faceted Palace formed the east side, and a new block of state and private apartments for the tsar with a passageway into the Grand Princes' Wing was put up on the west side.

In using this type of design, the builders were following the traditions of ancient Russian architecture. The new complex assimilated features from the Great Sovereign's Palace of the fifteenth to seventeenth centuries, which had also been a conglomeration of numerous and diverse structures. It was not only in borrowing the design of the old palace, however, that Thon and his associates turned to the traditions of Russian architecture, but also in attempting to give a lively impression of asymmetry to the exterior of the building. Thus, not all of its sections have the same length and height, the wings being lower than the main block. The Grand Princes' Wing was separated from the palace, as the quarters of the royal family with the outbuildings and churches had formerly been. The "hanging" passageway with a winter garden (built on arches) recalls such structures of olden times and the pattern of the arches on the façades seems to echo the arcade of Ivan III's palace. In silhouette, the roof of the main block conjures up associations with the *bochki**, *kokoshniki***, attics, and look-out towers on old Russian buildings. The projecting terrace of the main and east façades resembles traditional ambulatories, and the numerous windows are embellished with carved white limestone surrounds and a pendant typical of seventeenth-century Russian terems. All these devices were designed to help integrate the ancient structures of the Kremlin and the new palace in a single artistic whole. This use of tradition was not, however, simply a manifestation of professional skill on the part of the architect, but was dictated to a far greater extent by the official ideology of the Russian empire in the mid-nineteenth century, which was attempting to revive the so-called national or Russo-Byzantine artistic style, a style intended to glorify the autocratic power of the tsar and the

---

 * *Bochki*, arched stone roofs in the shape of cruciform barrels.
** *Kokoshniki*, a series of superimposed arches rising to a point (like the national Russian headdress *kokoshnik*), and framed by rich moulding.

Orthodox church as institutions which had supposedly always been part of Russian life and Russia's national identity. In architecture this was reflected in the desire to imitate Byzantine and old Russian churches. Thus, a completely modern palace with regard to layout, design and use of building materials, was decorated in the style of years long past.

In silhouette, the Great Kremlin Palace is simple but impressive; its solid main mass lends a monolithic appearance to the entire structure. This impression of unity is strengthened by the identically decorated façades with their rows of pilaster-strips and ornamental window surrounds. The main entrance does not stand out among the arches in the south façade. Although the palace has only two storeys, there are three rows of windows on the main façade, since the rooms on the upper floor have the windows arranged in two tiers.

Unlike the façades, the interiors of the palace have no direct analogies with the decor of old Russian buildings. Only the columns rising in spiral twists and the abundance of embellishments in the state rooms bring to mind the ornate style of the seventeenth century; most of the palace decor is done in the spirit of Classicism, with frequent architectural details in the Baroque style. This combination of styles probably suited Nicholas I's taste best, since it gave his residence a stately and festive look.

The decorations and furnishings of the Great Kremlin Palace, which have almost all survived to the present day, provide an extremely rare example of the mid-nineteenth century Russian palatial interior. All its artistic components are marked by an inner unity, a sense of cohesion and a superb craftsmanship. Besides Thon, the architects Richter, Chichagov and Bakarev, and the artist F. Solntsev were responsible for the creation of this decor. The archives of the State Museums in the Kremlin show how carefully all the details of the finish, decoration and furniture were thought out. Along with plans and views of entire apartments, many drawings and draughts were made of such fittings as fireplaces, chandeliers, candelabra, sconces, lamps, window lattices, stair-rails, doors, furniture, inlaid parquet floors, rugs, and painted ceilings. The plans show the general arrangement of the furnishings, while the cross-sections give more detail on the items themselves.

The Great Kremlin Palace is an artistic and historical landmark. It vividly reflects typical decorative methods and devices and contains under one roof representative items of the applied art of the day. At the same time the palace is a brilliant example of a new type of building in nineteenth-century Russian architecture. Its layout is more varied and integrated, with emphasis placed on comfort and functionality.

The palace builders employed many construction methods and materials which were novel and progressive for that time. Thon boldly introduced metal floor-beams, iron girders and a suspended ceiling, raised hollow zinc columns in the St George Hall, the largest of the state rooms, and used concrete, stone and cast iron floor-plates in the inner passageways and landings. The old Russian stoves were also replaced by a hot air heating system.

The architect made skilful use of varied decorative materials. He continued to employ the white limestone typical of buildings in the Kremlin, while introducing grey stone quarried not far from Moscow, granite from near Serdobol on the northern shore of Lake Ladoga and from Revel (now Tallinn), and also malachite and jasper from the Urals and Altai mountains.

The interiors of the Great Kremlin Palace were decorated by eminent Russian sculptors such as Ivan Vitali, Piotr Klodt and Alexander Loganovsky as well as the above-mentioned Richter, Chichagov, Solntsev, and Thon himself. Paintings on historical subjects were commissioned from the Russian artist F. Moller and the Frenchman Adolphe Yvon, and furniture and fitments were ordered from Russia's largest and best-known factories and workshops.

It took twelve years — from 1838 to 1849 — to build and fit out the palace, at a cost of eleven million roubles, which was an extremely large sum at the time. The last grandiose monument of nineteenth-century European palace architecture, it surpassed all other contemporary palaces in size and luxury. In accordance with old Russian custom, the palace was inaugurated, in April, 1849. A select number of guests received invitations to dinner and balls. The tables of the St Alexander Hall were laid with an antique dinner service, and along the wall stood *postavtsy*-containers covered with an array of old Russian and European jewelled plate, taken from the Armoury. As in olden times, the banqueting hall was resplendent with royal gold drinking-vessels encrusted with glimmering pearls and gems, goblets of sparkling crystal and glowing agate, and gold dishes polished to a brilliant shine. Tapers in antique candlesticks and wall-brackets shed their bright, flickering light against the shaded gilt walls. Noblemen, high-ranking officials and officers in dazzling uniforms sat next to ladies wearing gowns and high headgear cut to resemble sixteenth- or seventeenth-century Russian national dress.

The state rooms are arranged along the entire perimeter of the second floor. Named after old Russian orders, they are decorated accordingly: the crosses and stars of the order are repeated in the moulding, while the furniture is upholstered in fabric of the same colour as the ribbons of the order. The St George Hall was conceived and planned as a monument to the glory of Russian arms. The enormous proportions of this hall with its glittering white paintwork create an atmosphere of stateliness and grandeur. The commemorative character of this room is emphasized by the repetitive design incorporating the emblem of the order and the star with the device *For service and bravery*, and the names, inscribed in gold on marble, of distinguished regiments and the bearers of the order, amongst whom were such celebrated generals as Alexander Suvorov, Mikhail Kutuzov and Piotr Bagration, the famous admirals Fiodor Ushakov and Pavel Nakhimov as well as many heroes of the 1812 War.

The stately appearance of the room is enhanced by the multitude of mouldings, carvings, sculptures, and ormolu articles, and also by the variegated parquet floor designed by F. Solntsev and inlaid with more than twenty rare kinds of wood.

The St George Hall is 61 metres long, 20.5 wide and 17.5 high. Rectangular in plan, it has a coffered ceiling adorned with moulded plant ornament and rosettes. The east and south walls are set with two rows of windows. The austere noble aspect of the hall is created by the white and gold colour scheme. The vaulted ceiling rests on eighteen mighty pylons attached to hollow zinc columns. Rising in spiral twists, the latter are decorated with oak garlands and topped with ornate Corinthian capitals. The marble sculptures by Ivan Vitali placed on projecting cornices above the columns represent in allegorical form the provinces which had been incorporated into the Russian state from the late fifteenth to the early nineteenth century.

One of the best of these, *Little Russia*, symbolizes the voluntary union of the Ukraine and Russia in 1654. A majestic woman, full of nobility and dignity, holds a shield with a crest inscribed *1654* in her left hand and a mace, the symbol of the power of the *hetman*, ruler of the Ukraine, in her right. The figure is moulded in a laconic manner. The robe, draped in the ancient Greek fashion, falls in free folds. This statue is endowed with the classical simplicity characteristic of Vitali's finest works.

Many of the most important events in Soviet history have taken place in the St George Hall. In 1945 it played host to the participants of the Victory Parade, held in Red Square to mark the end of the Great Patriotic War against Nazi Germany. In 1947 the nation's highest award, the Order of Lenin, was presented here to a delegation of the working people of Moscow in honour of the capital's 800th anniversary. In 1961 Yuri Gagarin, the first man in space, was triumphally received here, and in 1956 and 1969 the hall was used for congresses of Communist and workers' parties.

The St Vladimir Hall, next to the St George Hall, is a square room with truncated corners and a faceted dome. It is small in area (about 16 metres square), but has a high ceiling: the distance from the floor to the glazed skylight in the centre of the dome is 18 metres. The walls are divided into two tiers; the lower comprises a rhythmic series of arched apertures, while the upper is decorated with smaller arches arranged in groups of three. Above the tiers there is a gallery encircling the hall, with several windows on its west side. The walls are faced with light-coloured imitation marble. The colour scheme on the lower section of the walls consists of harmonious shades of white, pink and light green. All the lavish decor is concentrated on the dome, covered with gilded stuccowork executed by the serf craftsmen Fiodor and Nikolai Dylev. The floral designs include emblems of the order, a cross and a star with the device *For honour, glory and the public good*.

The dome of the St Vladimir Hall is remarkable not only for its decor but also for its successful technical and constructive design. It is made from hollow ceramic pots, which relieve pressure and improve the acoustics of the room. The dome is crowned with a glass skylight 6 metres high through which sunlight streams in. A large ormolu chandelier weighing 740 kg, with two hundred small lamps arranged in three tiers, hangs from the skylight on a metal rope directly over the central rosette of the parquet floor, inlaid with dark fumed oak and variously shaded walnut.

The St Vladimir Hall was intended for a specific purpose: to form a link between the palace's halls and chambers built at various times. Only through

Видъ Кремлевскаго стараго | Vue du vieux Palais de Tsar
дворца съ Краснымъ крыль- | dans le Kreml avec le grand
цомъ и Золотою решетиою | Escalier et la grille d'or.

II. *The Terem Palace, Golden Porch, Boyar Gathering-place and Cathedral of Our Saviour (Verkhospassky). Engraving from a drawing by M. Makhayev. 1760s*

it one can reach the fifteenth-century Faceted Palace, the sixteenth-century Tsarina's Golden Chamber and Zhiletskaya Chamber, or climb to the seventeenth-century Terem Palace. The specific layout of the St Vladimir Hall is determined by the peculiarities of the site on which it was built. In the past, in the inner yard amongst the mass of fifteenth- to seventeenth-century buildings, between the large reception rooms and living quarters, and right next to the Private Bedchambers, stood the porch leading to the Bedchambers. In the seventeenth century, boyars, noblemen and officials having business in the palace would gather in front of the porch to hear news and the tsar's decrees.

The St Vladimir Hall is now used for the signing of important international documents. During Party congresses, national and international conferences and sessions of the Supreme Soviet, the deputies, delegates and guests rest here between meetings. The hall also accommodates guests during large receptions. In 1961 Soviet architects took advantage of its key position to construct a passageway from the old palace to the new Palace of Congresses and to lay out the new Winter Garden in the Great Palace.

The Winter Garden, opened shortly before the beginning of 1960, is situated on the second floor. The main access to the garden is from the St Vladimir

Вид новаго дворца въ | Façade du nouveau Palais
Кремлѣ съ Южной стороны. | Imperial dans le Kreml
vers le midi.

III. *The South Façade of the Kremlin Palace (1749–1753). Engraving from a drawing by* M. *Makhayev. 1760s*

Hall. It covers 320 square metres, of which 110 square metres is taken up by tropical and subtropical plants. Constant temperature and humidity are maintained by means of an air conditioning system. Flooded with daylight, the garden is adorned with vases and statues, and has a mosaic pond with a fountain and goldfish. This Garden is one of the cosiest corners of the palace. The St Catherine Hall takes its name from the Order of St Catherine, established by Peter the Great in 1714, and previously served as a throne room for the Russian empresses. Its ceiling is formed of groin vaults supported by two massive pylons. The hall is relatively small but has an air of both stateliness and tranquillity.

The colour scale is dominated by light colours, with a white ceiling and walls hung with silvery moire, but in places touches of gilt and bright red and green are introduced. Red is repeated in the emblems decorating the hall, the ribbons of the order bordering the rectangular moire panels on the walls, and the marble supports of the huge crystal candelabra. Green malachite is used on the pilasters of the pylons and those in the corners of the hall, while the mouldings on the ceiling, the ornamental designs on the doors, and the bronze capitals of the pilasters are gilded. The stuccowork on the vaults, the artificial marble facing of the friezes and pylons, the malachite mosaic on the pilasters, the skilfully carved doors with emblems and plant designs covered with a thick layer of gilt, and the austere and noble forms of the furniture made in the spirit of Late Russian Classicism all betray the talent and subtle artistic taste of nineteenth-century Russian craftsmen.

The St Catherine Hall is now used for meetings of various committees of the Supreme Soviet, receptions of foreign parliamentary delegations and heads of state, and presentation of the highest state awards.

The Hall is bordered on the south by the former Chevalier Guard's Room and on the north by the State Drawing Room, the State Bedchamber and, finally, the Walnut Cloak Room, which together make up the State Apartments occupying the entire west wing of the palace, located at right angles to the main block. A large mirror hangs on the end wall of the Walnut Cloak Room. Placed at the very end of the suite, the mirror not only reflects the several preceding rooms, but also creates the illusion of a chain of halls stretching into the distance.

The Chevalier Guard's Room, where the tsar's personal bodyguards formerly kept watch, is the first room in the suite. Its decor is marked by economy and austerity, with white walls faced to resemble marble and doors of light planewood.

The spacious and luxuriously furnished State Drawing Room (Divan Room) has a high vaulted ceiling decorated with light-coloured plant designs by the Italian Giuseppe Colombo Artari. The walls are hung with patterned green and gold brocade which matches the brocade upholstery of the soft furniture, inlaid with bronze, mother-of-pearl and tortoise-shell plates. The high rosewood doors set with mirrors are also inlaid with exquisite patterns.

Various bronze and porcelain items complement the furniture and fittings; the most striking among them are the large, intricately shaped and gaily painted porcelain standard lamp with sixty-six candlesticks and vases for fresh flowers, and also two candelabra in the Japanese and Chinese style. Almost all the porcelain in the Great Palace, including the pieces just mentioned, was made at the famous Imperial Porcelain Factory in St Petersburg.

The State Bedchamber leading from the State Drawing Room contains an alcove with monolithic columns hewed out of grey-green marble, an invariable feature of such rooms. The expanse of wall is broken up by pilasters, some of which are faced in the same marble and some in artificial marble of a similar shade. The fireplace is tiled with deep greenish-blue jasper in a rare smoky shade. The Bedchamber was originally dominated by these somewhat cold colours, which harmonized well with the walls, upholstered in silver brocade with gold patterns. Later, in the 1880s, the light brocade was replaced by crimson damask, and gilded furniture with soft quilted upholstery in the same material appeared.

The former Private Apartments of the tsar are decorated no less richly than the State Apartments. They have great artistic value as a veritable museum of nineteenth-century Russian decorative and applied art. The living quarters on the first floor extend along the main façade, forming a suite with the windows on the south side. There are seven main rooms: the Dining Room, the Empress' Drawing Room and Study, the Boudoir, the Bedroom, the Emperor's Reception Room and Study, and four sitting rooms for the secretary, courtiers and ladies-in-waiting.

All these rooms are spacious and high-ceilinged, and most of them are supported by a massive pier at the front, which not only holds up the ceiling but also allows the division of the room into small, cosy compartments.

The Private Apartments, like the state halls, contain furniture specially manufactured for the purpose. They house a fine collection of bronzes, crystal, porcelains, fabrics, and *objets d'art* cut from coloured semi-precious stones. In every hall and room the stucco mouldings, the artificial marble facings, the decorative parquet floors, and the inlaid furniture are distinguished by a high level of craftsmanship. The interiors of the Private Apartments clearly reflect the stylistic variety which is one of the most typical features of the Great Kremlin Palace as a whole. indeed, the private suite runs the gamut of styles from Classicism to Baroque or elegant Rococo.

The first and largest of the Private Apartments is the Dining Room, into which daylight streams through four high arched windows. The room is further brightened by its predominantly white colour scheme and the glossy sheen of the artificial marble which covers the walls and central supporting pylon. Since the Dining Room is about twice as big as any succeeding room, this pylon is likewise more massive; there are white marble niches in its broad sides as well as in the end walls of the room which contain marble vases with reliefs on mythological subjects and statues of Hymen, the Greek God of marriage, and the beautiful Leda, beloved of Zeus.

In the decor of this room, the architect let his fancy roam freely, blending antique motifs with Renaissance elements. Therefore, classical features such as marble walls divided into coloured panels, niches, marble statues, vases, and Roman-style floor lamps are in accord with popular Renaissance elements, arches, pilasters and a finely profiled cornice. Renaissance motifs, though much more freely interpreted, also occur in the furniture and the mouldings which enliven the stark whiteness of the ceiling.

The following apartment, the Empress' Drawing Room, reflects the capricious grace of the Rococo style. This is seen in the light colour scheme, made up of soft white, pink, pale blue and gold; in the lively elegance of the moulded and painted floral designs, and in the elaborate, wavy contours of the furniture. At the same time, the geometrically patterned plafond, the strictly oval medallions with bas-relief depictions of *Morning, Evening, Day,* and *Night,* and the rhythmically alternating smooth pilasters all betray the influence of Classicism. Porcelain is an important element in the decoration of this room which is filled with vases, table lamps, and candelabra. The "pineapple chandelier", a large central chandelier with decorative china pineapples on its top and base, is embellished with an array of porcelain flowers, painted and moulded so skilfully that they almost seem natural.

The Empress' Study is decorated in the style of French palace apartments of the late seventeenth and early eighteenth centuries. It abounds in white and coloured marble, gilt, bronze, crystal, mirrors, and expensive fabrics. The

IV. *The Boyar Gathering-place, Terem Palace, Golden Porch and Cathedral of Our Saviour (Verkhospassky). Water-colour by F. Alexeyev. 1800*

walls are hung with crimson brocade, and the upholstery and heavy window drapes are of patterned silk in the same shade. The floor is covered with a soft carpet with a dense floral ornament against a crimson ground. The dark walnut and rosewood furniture with ormolu mounts is inlaid with tortoise-shell and bronze plaques, sometimes interspersed with mother-of-pearl and varicoloured wood. This style is known as buhlwork from the name of its inventor, André Charles Boulle, cabinet-maker to the French king.

The appointments of the study give little indication as to its purpose; the bookcases and writing-desk go almost unnoticed amidst soft furniture more appropriate for a drawing room. However, it is precisely this group of cabinet furniture, together with an antique clock and doors inset with ormolu, tortoise-shell and mother-of-pearl, that bears witness to the fine workmanship of the Russian cabinet-makers of the time.

The Empress' Boudoir has a typical nineteenth-century Russian interior influenced by no particular style. The subtle combination of pink, greenish-grey and silver adds elegance and calm beauty to the Boudoir. As the fashion of the period demanded, the walls of the Boudoir are upholstered identically in patterned silk, creating a uniform background against which the dark polished walnut furniture makes an effective contrast. The neatly arranged furniture with its soft quilted upholstery in the Gambs style gives an impression of comfort, offsetting the large dimensions of the room.

V. *The Kremlin Palace (1749–1753). Belfry of Ivan the Great, Cathedral of the Archangel Michael and Church of the Annunciation by the Kremlin Wall. Water-colour by F. Alexeyev. 1800*

Between the two windows in the front half of the Boudoir there is a fireplace which seems to have been cut from one block of stone but is in fact tiled with thin pieces of malachite; its striking monolithic appearance is entirely due to the painstakingly crafted mosaic.

The furnishings of the Emperor's Bedroom and Study were chosen to suit the rooms' purpose. The Study looks severe and official, and its furniture is totally functional: two huge desks, chairs and a small narrow sofa, all of light Karelian birch upholstered in green cloth and Morocco leather. The walls are panelled in light ash; one of the panels conceals the bookcase which used to hold the code of laws of the Russian Empire. The room is soundproofed effectively by its cavity walls.

The last of the Private Apartments is the Emperor's Reception Room, the decor of which deserves particular attention. The soft furniture resembles drawing-room pieces. The sofas and armchairs are upholstered in a "velvet on satin" material in gold, brown and green. The floral pattern in velvet pile stands out against the smooth satiny background, and the pile is specially cut to allow a rich play of light and shade. This beautiful upholstery material, along with most of that used for the palace, was woven at the factory of G. Sapozhnikov, a Moscow merchant.

As has already been mentioned, the complex of the Great Kremlin Palace designed by Konstantin Thon incorporated structures from previous centuries.

The earliest of these is the Faceted Palace (*Granovitaya Palata*), one of the most important monuments of Russian architecture and the oldest secular building in the Kremlin. Its main or east façade, which overlooks Cathedral Square, is laid with white faceted stone, hence the name. The palace was built between 1487 and 1491 by the Milanese architects Pietro Antonio Solari and Marco Ruffo. Its exterior shows elements of the late Italian Gothic style favoured by many northern Italian builders at the time: the solid cubic volume, the lancet double-windows and the slender corner colonnettes.

The Faceted Palace is well integrated with the other Kremlin structures. Its contemporaries were impressed by its clarity and unity of form, harmonious proportions and affinity with the national architectural tradition. The layout of the palace is akin to that of a Russian home of the period; the entrance to the main building is an echo of the entrance-hall customary in Russian houses. The two-storey building stands on a high basement. The state hall on the second floor has a ceiling resting on groin vaults supported by a huge central pier.

For fifteenth-century Muscovites, the Faceted Palace was a brilliant feat of architecture, because such a spacious, tall and well-lit hall had never been seen before. The palace is 495 sq. metres in area with a height of 9 metres and walls more than 1.5 metres thick. It is almost square in plan, with a pier in the centre. Rays of light penetrate the room freely from three sides through eighteen windows of varying size and shape, arranged in two tiers. In 1684, when the palace was being repaired and renovated after a major fire, the craftsman Osip Startsev widened the lower tier of windows and embellished them on the outside with carved white limestone surrounds, of which those on the main façade are especially intricate and ornate. At the same time the roof was laid with an iron sheeting with brightly coloured designs painted on a gold background. The sheeting, unfortunately, has not survived to the present day.

In general, the palace is extremely well preserved, and relatively few changes have been made during the past centuries. The four-slope roof was lowered and refurbished, and the ancient main stairway (the so-called Red Porch) demolished. These stairs once adjoined the south wall on the outside and led from Cathedral Square to the porch and entrance-hall of the Faceted Palace. In 1954 the façade was cleaned off and thus was returned to its original appearance.

The interior of the palace has changed numerous times as the various names for the building to a certain extent prove. Originally it was called the Great Chamber, then, after the fire of 1547, the Great Golden Faceted Chamber. Later, at the end of the sixteenth century, under Tsar Fiodor, it was renamed the Great Golden Painted Chamber, since it was first decorated with murals done on a gold background. Each new title reflected the most salient features of its decor in each particular period.

In the Faceted Palace foreign ambassadors were received and state sessions held. It was also the scene of *zemsky sobors,* assemblies of representatives from various estates in Old Russia. Here, in 1552, Ivan the Terrible celebrated

VI. *View of the Kremlin from the Stone Bridge. 1825 lithograph from a late 18th-century drawing by Cadolle.*

his victory over the Khanate of Kazan; in 1649 the Assembly discussed the issue of union between Russia and the Ukraine; in 1709 Peter the Great held a reception to mark his triumph over the Swedes at Poltava, and trophies won in the battle were displayed in the palace.

In the fifteenth to seventeenth centuries it was customary to celebrate the birth of a child or a name-day in the tsar's family with a grandiose feast for boyars and important members of the clergy in the palace, and in the eighteenth and nineteenth centuries coronation dinners were held there. On such occasions the hall was especially lavishly decorated. Persian rugs and swathes of valuable coloured fabric were spread on the floor, squares of silver and gold material covered the benches, and a large quantity of precious plate was laid out on the tables. The main decoration in the palace was the large royal *postavets*-container. Open, pyramid-shaped and placed around the central pier, it groaned under the weight of gold and silver vessels of the most amazing forms and sizes. Many of these are now on show in the Kremlin Armoury.

The chronicles record that the walls of the Faceted Palace were painted with murals in the late sixteenth century. These frescoes were unusual in that they combined biblical subjects and scenes illustrating religious legends and parables with historical and everyday themes, so-called true stories. One of the earliest known Russian portraits, a representation of Tsar Fiodor, was painted on the south wall. Unfortunately, the early frescoes of the Faceted Palace have not survived. On several occasions during the seventeenth century the walls were painted over, and in the eighteenth century the murals were demolished along with the plaster and replaced by red velvet embroidered with coats of arms in gold thread.

The interior then remained as it was until late in the nineteenth century. In 1882 the Palekh painters Belousov recreated the frescoes according to a detailed description of the originals made in 1672 by the famous royal icon-painter Simon Ushakov. Keeping as close as possible to Ushakov's account, the brothers Belousov reproduced scenes from the Bible and Russian history on the walls and vaults of the palace. The subjects depicted include the legend of the creation of the universe, the creation and fall of Adam and Eve and their expulsion from Eden; the story of Joseph; scenes from the life of King David and King Solomon; and the parable of the just and unjust judges. On the window bevellings and the lateral parts of the east and south walls there are depictions of old Russian princes and tsars; scenes showing Vladimir Monomachus receiving the cross and royal insignia from the envoys of the Byzantine Emperor Constantine; and a representation of Prince Vladimir teaching his twelve sons how to live righteously and rule wisely.

Between the first and second windows of the south wall there is a composition showing Tsar Fiodor, son of Ivan the Terrible. Surrounded by his favoured boyars and clergymen, the young tsar is seated on the throne in full panoply, his orb and sceptre in his hands. Of all the ancient murals in the palace, this scene served a special purpose: it reflected the basically worldly character and political import of the paintings. Next to the throne, at the tsar's right hand, stands Boris Godunov, Fiodor's most trusted counsellor who in fact ruled Russia at the time and gained the throne after Fiodor's death. On the opposite wall are compositions on the biblical legend of Joseph, whose rise to power was seen as an allegorical parallel to that of Godunov.

The murals which the brothers Belousov executed in the Faceted Palace manifest the basic stylistic features of the Palekh school such as the prevalence of narrative element, interest in thematic detail, decorativeness, enclosed areas of colour, and well-designated outline. In addition, the artists fused together the academic canons of painting and the Palekh tradition of icon-painting by combining the realistic treatment of forms with the two-dimensionality and ornamentality characteristic of icons.

The Belousov murals have survived in extremely good condition. They only needed a cleaning in 1949 and another during the major restoration of the palace in 1968. Also at that time extensive research had made it possible to reconstruct the ancient gilded carving of the central pier and to renew the decor of the white limestone portal—the backgrounds were painted brick-red and the carved relief on the pier was regilded.

On the west side the Faceted Palace adjoins a spacious vestibule above which there is a small secret room with a single window facing into the palace. The women of the royal family presumably used this window to observe what took place in the hall, for contemporary etiquette did not permit them to be present at state receptions. The first woman to appear publicly in the Faceted

Palace was the Tsarina Sophia, the elder sister and regent of the young Tsars Ivan and Peter. (The two boys reigned together, and their unique double throne, which once stood in the palace, is now kept in the Armoury.) The ambitious and energetic Sophia boldly defied the ancient restrictions. She even had a special room, built in her maiden's quarters, to receive foreign ambassadors and, in 1682, she entered the palace to take part in a debate on faith with the Old Believers, whose leader, Nikita Pustosviat, was later put to death on her orders.

The entrance-hall of the Faceted Palace has long since been called the Holy Antechamber: its walls are decorated with murals of an entirely religious character and it was traditionally compared with the similar antechamber to the state room in the royal palace in Byzantium. It was through the Holy Antechamber that the Russian tsars made public appearances during coronations and important religious ceremonies.

The Holy Antechamber acquired its present-day aspect in the 1840s, when Konstantin Thon extended it on the north side at the expense of the adjacent structures and added two new carved and gilded interior portals to the existing pair. The three windows on the west wall which formerly overlooked the Boyar Gathering-place, opposite the entrance to the Faceted Palace, were demolished, and a door linking the Holy Antechamber with the St Vladimir Hall in the Great Palace was put up. The carved inscription above the ancient portal where the Red Porch once stood was renovated. It states that the foundations of the Faceted Palace and its Holy Antechamber were laid in 1487 during the reign of Ivan the Great. Above the only window still surviving in the Holy Antechamber there is another inscription about the remodelling of the building in 1847 during the reign of Nicholas I.

The ancient frescoes in the Holy Antechamber have not survived, and the existing murals were executed in 1847−49 by Fiodor Zavyalov, Academician of Painting. He restored the religious pictures according to Ushakov's description, then painted two murals on themes from Russian history: *St Sergius of Radonezh Blessing Prince Dmitry Donskoi before the Battle of Kulikovo* and *The Grand Prince Vladimir of Kiev Accepting the Christian Faith.*

Next to the Faceted Palace stands another ancient palatial structure. It is first mentioned in late sixteenth-century records as the Golden Chamber of the Tsarina Irina, the wife of Fiodor. The chamber is rectangular in plan and built on a high arched basement. The arches are clearly visible from Cathedral Square (between the Faceted Palace and the Church of the Deposition of the Robe). The exterior of the Golden Chamber is most admired for its Renaissance features: the profiled carved cornice, the beaded Ionic ornamental designs and the intricate carving over the portal. Since the construction of the Great Kremlin Palace, the Tsarina's Golden Chamber has been walled in from three sides, and only its east façade now gives on to Cathedral Square. The two windows on the south side which formerly overlooked the Boyar Gathering-place now face directly into the St Vladimir Hall.

The Tsarina's Chamber is less spacious than the Faceted Palace: it is smaller in area and with lower vaults. The original interior decor was distorted at the end of the seventeenth century by new stone arches and tie-bars. The two cross arches extending from wall to wall, and the tie-bars were needed to reinforce the chamber vaults, which had become overburdened with the weight of the structures above: the Cathedral of Our Saviour (Verkhospassky), built in 1636, and the Church of the Crucifixion, built in 1681. The Golden Portal of the Tsarina's Chamber opening into the Zhiletskaya Chamber is adorned with intertwined Italianate gilt patterns.

In the 1580s the Tsarina's Golden Chamber was decorated with frescoes painted on a gold background, hence the name of the building. During the seventeenth and eighteenth centuries they were renewed several times, always in accordance with the original compositions. These paintings depict scenes from the life of Christian tsarinas and princesses of the fourth to ninth centuries who were famous for their wisdom and virtue, such as Helena, Irine and Theodora; the legendary Georgian Queen Tamar (late 12th and early 13th centuries); and the Russian princess Olga (10th century). In these murals emphasis is placed on various everyday objects. This can best be seen in the mural on the east wall, where the artist pays special attention to the carriage in which Princess Olga and her boyars are setting out from Kiev for Constantinople.

Two original pieces dating back to 1588–89 have been restored on the north wall by Soviet experts. The first is a fragment of a mural painted on gold, discovered in 1925 when part of a seventeenth-century arch was pulled down; the second, cleaned in 1947, is part of a multifigure composition symbolizing the triumph of the Christian host. The galloping riders, wielding lances and decked in figured robes, full armour and helmets, advance in close formation behind their leader, who rides ahead on a white horse. The mural has a balanced rhythm and beautiful colour scheme. All the other murals in the chamber were uncovered in 1978 and date from the seventeenth century.

In olden times the Tsarina's Golden Chamber was the state reception room of the Russian tsarinas. Here in 1589 the Tsarina Irina received Jeremiah, Patriarch of Constantinople, and Bishop Arsenius, who arrived in Russia to attend the ceremony marking the foundation of an independent patriarchate. Arsenius gives us the earliest account of the chamber, from which the interior decor of the period can partially be reconstructed. He writes that the walls and vault were suffused with gold and radiated light, coloured murals glowed on the walls, the gems in the icon-frames shed a thousand sparks, the Persian carpets underfoot shone with golden silk, and the niches and window-sills gleamed with ceremonial vessels and fanciful sculptured figures.

Adjacent to the Tsarina's Golden Chamber is the Zhiletskaya Chamber. It served as quarters for the palace guard, a body of lesser-ranking noblemen, called *zhiltsy*, hence the name. Two of the most interesting features of this hall are the stone window surround and the seventeenth-century portal, both of which, along with the two windows in the Tsarina's Golden Chamber, overlook the St Vladimir Hall.

In former times the tsar's living quarters were on the north side of the rectangle formed by the palace buildings; their main section, the Terem

Palace has survived to this day. The Palace was built in 1635–36 by the Russian stone-masons Antip Konstantinov, Trephil Sharutin, Bazhen Ogurtsov, and Larion Ushakov for Tsar Mikhail Romanov, Peter the Great's grandfather.

The Terem Palace represents the first attempt at building a stone residence in the Kremlin. As its composition, layout and decoration clearly show, it was constructed along the lines of old wooden houses. The unusually shaped structure, with floors rising in tiers; the sharply pointed roofs of the main section; the porches; the rooms which resemble frames of logs placed side by side; and the obligatory three windows on the façade in each room — all owe their origins to Russian wooden architecture. Carving, which dominates the decoration, was also a tribute to the old traditions of wooden architecture. At the same time, the Terem Palace played an important part in the development of stone architecture in Russia; after its construction rich Muscovites began to erect their own stone houses in the areas adjacent to the Kremlin.

The Terem Palace is a high building. On its fifth floor is an attic or *teremok*, which later gave its name to the entire structure. The first two storeys have survived from the palace put up between 1499 and 1508 and from the workshops built in the sixteenth century during the reign of Ivan the Terrible. The three higher storeys, which date from the seventeenth century, are arranged in ascending tiers characteristic of Russian architecture at that period. Gradually diminishing in size, the floors almost seem to sprout one from another; each successive storey rests on the vaults of the one below and is set back from its outer walls. The space thus created is laid with circular open terraces-promenades, and wide landings in front of the entrances.

The architecture of the Terem Palace is striking in its exuberance. The façades feature fully profiled cornices, pilasters, and lavishly ornamented portals and window surrounds. The latter were particularly sumptuously carved in tune with the Russian builders' growing awareness that the window could not only serve a functional purpose but also be used as an architectural element with great decorative potential. The most opulent window of all is that in the Tsar's Study. It has a high pediment decorated with a coat of arms and supported by two colonnettes with sculptures of reclining lions at their base. Legend has it that in olden days a box into which complaints and requests could be placed, supposedly for the tsar's immediate attention, was periodically lowered into the courtyard of the Terem Palace from this window. However, the requests were not answered for a long time and the tsar's "long box" became a joke amongst the citizens, hence the Russian expression "to put the matter in a long box" or "to put it off till kingdom come".

The windows of the palace were no more finely decorated than the portals, with their fancifully shaped lintels and abundance of carved white limestone ornament. Popular Russian grass designs, heraldic motifs, birds, animals, masks, and human figures all blend into varicoloured lacy patterns against the stark white of the limestone.

The Golden Porch, the main entrance to the Terem Palace, is on the terrace of the Cathedral of Our Saviour. The porch was called "Golden" because of

VII. *The St Andrew Hall of the Great Kremlin Palace.*
Water-colour by K. Ukhtomsky. 1849

its opulence; it was not only painted but also copiously gilded. The carved
limestone steps leading to the palace are interspersed with landings, surmounted by gay tent roofs. The latter rest on faceted pylons linked by rampant
arches with pendants. The parapets of the stairway are decorated with stone
lions. As one of the most important elements of the old Russian house, the
porch was constructed in the best traditions of both masonry and carpentry.
In 1847–49, when the Golden Porch was already inside the Great Kremlin
Palace, Timofei Kiseliov decorated it with new murals. Fragments of ancient
compositions, uncovered in the 1850s and 60s, can also be seen on the porch.
The Terem Palace has undergone no radical architectural changes. However,
over the more than three and a half centuries of its existence it has naturally
experienced some mishaps. In 1812, when officers of Napoleon's army were
quartered there, the furniture was broken or burnt, the precious cloth and
silver stolen, and the murals severely damaged. In the 1830s, the interior was
reconstructed. Fiodor Richter, who was in charge of the restoration, made use

VIII. *The St Alexander Hall of the Great Kremlin Palace. Water-colour by K. Ukhtomsky. 1849*

of traditional Russian motifs in the decor, reinstalled the surviving antique furniture and reupholstered new chairs in old velvet. Many objects were refurbished according to seventeenth-century samples, including the carved window-sills, the oak *postavtsy*-containers inset with glazed figured frames, and the multicoloured tiled stoves. The ornamental window frames fitted with variegated mica were replaced by oak ones set with stained glass, and the furniture was arranged in the traditional manner.

The interior as well as the exterior of the palace abounds with ornamentation of various kinds. The intricate stone carving on the outside harmonizes with that on the wooden window-sills and furniture; the multicoloured ceramic tiles at the top of the external walls match the tiles of the stoves in the inner rooms, and the colour scheme of the walls and porches echoes the bright decorative paintings inside.

There is much information, albeit fragmentary, about the ancient murals of the Terem Palace. According to one account, the Throne Room was painted

IX. *The State Bedchamber of the Great Kremlin Palace. Water-colour by K. Ukhtomsky. 1849*

in 1644, during the reign of Tsar Mikhail, after which it was renamed the Sovereign's Golden Chamber. We know that during the second half of the seventeenth century, a group of painters led by Simon Ushakov decorated the palace with murals, which were subsequently touched up or completely repainted on several occasions. The existing oil-paintings were done by Timofei Kiseliov in 1836—38 after drawings by Solntsev. They are dominated by plant designs and scenes on religious subjects.

The Terem Palace is interesting not only as an architectural monument but also as a living chronicle of an era long gone. Each of the floors had its own way of life. The basement contained various kinds of cellars and store-rooms where in the seventeenth century wine and vodka were kept, candles stored, honey and wax made, and various foods laid by. Here *sbeeten* (Russian popular drink, composed of hot water and honey) was brewed, apples preserved in molasses, and vegetables and fruits salted and soaked. The steward's office was also on this floor. The storey above housed the Tsarina's Workshops in which clothes, covers, bed-curtains, and sled-rugs were sewn, all expertly and intricately embroidered with silk, gold and pearls. The Workshops were also used to store all kinds of garments, linen, and clothes for the tsar and his family. The third floor was occupied by some minor living rooms and various offices and servants' quarters. These rooms are small, with vaulted ceilings and deeply recessed windows. In the reign of Tsar Mikhail, the game-room of the small Prince Alexei was on this floor, and in the 1670s a "little washroom", or bath, was installed for the tsar in one of the distant rooms. Water was drawn up by means of a machine in one of the Kremlin towers, which is called the Water-tower to this day. In the nineteenth century, some rooms on this level housed the Archives where the most important state documents of former times were kept.

The fourth floor of the palace, where the tsar's private quarters were situated, is in the best state of preservation. Its layout is quite simple: small rooms of almost equal size are arranged along the façade looking south. Each of them has three windows and almost all contain tiled stoves. Benches and chairs are arrayed along the walls. These rooms do not exactly form a suite, for the doorways of the adjacent rooms do not lie on one axis.

The Anteroom was used by a few boyars who were close to the tsar and had access to his private quarters. They were obliged to appear there early each morning to welcome the tsar. Any absence without a valid excuse might call forth the sovereign's displeasure which he first showed by not sending the offender food from the royal table. Refreshments were sometimes served in the Anteroom, hence its alternative name, the Refectory.

The second room is known as the Cross, or Assembly Room. The Boyar Duma, which dealt with government affairs and various disputes between boyars, held its meetings there. Very seldom, as a sign of special goodwill and pleasure, the tsar received foreign ambassadors in this room. Such private, unofficial visit was equivalent to a gala farewell banquet in one of the ambassadors' chambers in the Great Sovereign's Palace.

The third room on this floor, the Sovereign's Room or Throne Room where the tsar's throne was kept, was the only one actually called a "room" in olden days. It functioned as a study where the tsar spent most of his time.

Occasionally it was used for intimate dinners at which a few guests close to the tsar could sit where they wished without being obliged to follow the rigid etiquette of rank and birth that was compulsory at other times. Next to the Throne Room was the Pantry from which the dishes were served up.

The Throne Room was the scene of important historical events. In 1660 a religious court met there to try Patriarch Nikon, who had attempted, by means of church reform, to make the temporal power of the patriarch equal to that of the tsar. The court's decision was to deprive Nikon of his "honour and the patriarch's seat".

The Throne Room is the most elegant room in the entire palace. The walls and ceiling are painted gold against a red background with plant designs, coats of arms of various cities and provinces in Russia and figures of saints. The tsar's throne, padded with velvet, stands in the forecorner, directly opposite a carved wooden dresser for crockery. Benches and chairs upholstered in crimson velvet are set along the walls, and in front of the windows there is a table on ornate figured legs with a painted tabletop and a gilded platform. The decor of the room is complemented by the large, round stove inlaid with attractive red tiles patterned in white, blue and green.

The last of the rooms on the fourth floor is the Bedchamber, in the centre of which stands a carved wooden four-poster bed with a canopy. The Bedchamber leads into the Oratory that contains two carved, gilded iconostases with seventeenth- and eighteenth-century icons.

The only room on the fifth floor is known as the Stone Attic, or Teremok. Spacious and well lit, it is distinguished by the richness and subtlety of its carved decor, done in white limestone. Above the entrance there is an inscription saying that the room was built by Tsar Mikhail for his children, Alexei and Ivan. The room is surrounded by an open terrace with a parapet accommodating a small watch-tower. In the seventeenth century this terrace was called the Upper Stone Yard and functioned as a play area for the royal children. It is accessible via two staircases located on opposite sides of the living quarters. The wide northeast staircase, with its right-angled turns and old carved steps and landings, was restored and repainted in the nineteenth century. The narrow spiral stairway on the southwest side, leading to the Teremok and Watch-tower, has changed little over the centuries so that the modern viewer can fully appreciate the beauty of the raised carvings on the white limestone steps and landings. The Watch-tower afforded a panorama of the city with its rabbit-warren of streets, tree-lined gardens, golden-domed churches, and monastery belfries with their tall, elegant spires. Soaring high above the crenellated walls of the Kremlin, the peaked tower and the cupolas of the palace churches were visible from afar.

The Terem Palace was only a small part of the extensive complex which made up the men's quarters of the seventeenth-century Great Sovereign's Palace. The women's quarters were always in a separate building; thus, in 1674 a grand house was put up to the north of the Terem Palace for Natalya Kirillovna, the mother of Peter the Great. In 1679 this house was remodelled and extended, but in 1749, during the construction of Rastrelli's palace, the site was levelled and later built up again. Now it is occupied by the Palace of Congresses.

The children's quarters were also divided according to the sexes and stood apart. Each section of the palace in any way independent of the others developed its own outbuildings, service-rooms, workshops, and churches. The architectural complex of the Great Kremlin Palace includes six churches: the Cathedral of Our Saviour, the Church of the Crucifixion, the Church of the Resurrection Glorified (*Voskresenie Slovoushchie*), St Catherine's Church, the Church of the Nativity of the Virgin, and the Church of the Raising of Lazarus.

The Church of the Raising of Lazarus (1393) is the oldest surviving building in Moscow and one of the unique monuments of white stone architecture in the Kremlin dating from the fourteenth century. Despite later renovations and distortions, the church gives a clear impression of the architectural style of that time. Put together from large rectangular blocks of white limestone, each up to thirty centimetres high, it is a cubic structure somewhat elongated from east to west, a layout characteristic of early Moscow buildings. This domed church, cruciform in plan, has one cupola and three apses. Four huge piers,

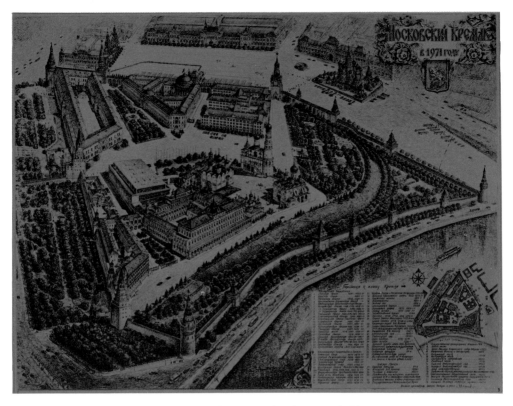

X. *The Moscow Kremlin. Axonometric projection by A. Khamtsov. 1971*

two square and two round, support the vaults. The round piers in the
western half of the church are surmounted by arches that in turn support the
choir. Within the wall, which is more than 1.5 metres thick, there is a
built-in staircase leading to the choir. The entrance to this staircase and also
the niches in the southwest pier and west wall have archivolts with ogee tops.
This design is repeated on the west portal, which closely resembles the
recessed doorways of churches in Vladimir and Suzdal. Indeed, the churches
in those ancient cities served as a prototype for Moscow architecture in the
fourteenth and fifteenth centuries. The entranceway is framed by the colonnettes decorated with alternating and braided mouldings.
The Church of the Raising of Lazarus, built in 1393, collapsed in 1479,
when, according to the chronicle, the roof fell in, the icons were damaged,
and vessels in great number belonging to the Grand Prince were broken. The
building was later restored and redecorated, but by the early sixteenth
century it had become part of the crypt of the new palace erected by Ivan
the Great and Vasily III and was thus forgotten for many centuries. In 1514
the Church of the Nativity of the Virgin, designed by Alevisio Novi, was
constructed above it. This later church was also refurbished numerous times;
the vault was rebuilt, and at the end of the seventeenth century its five
cupolas were replaced by a single one on a high drum. The interior, too,

underwent alterations. When Thon's Great Kremlin Palace was completed, the church was totally hidden from view. The only thing now visible from outside is its four-slope roof and small gilded cupola.

St Catherine's Church, erected in 1627 by the architect John Tahler, has undergone particularly extensive alterations. Built near the Tsarina's Golden Chamber, it is one of the group of house-chapels adjoining the Terem Palace on the east side. In olden days it was the main church serving the women's quarters, but in the seventeenth century it was already surrounded by several other structures and fell into obscurity. Its interior was radically remodelled in the mid-nineteenth century by Thon and Solntsev. Soviet experts have partially restored the building to its original state by uncovering and refurbishing the ancient connecting gallery and the north porch.

Other churches adjoining the Terem Palace on the east include the Cathedral of Our Saviour, the Church of the Crucifixion and the Church of the Resurrection Glorified. These three churches located on the upper floors of the palace are adjacent to the living quarters and in former times were called "the upper churches on top of the Sovereign's Anteroom".

The Cathedral of Our Saviour, together with its side chapel, was constructed at the same time as the Terem Palace (1635–36) by Bazhen Ogurtsov, Antip Konstantinov, Trephil Sharutin, and Larion Ushakov. Its entrance lies on the front stone courtyard, as does the Golden Porch of the Terem Palace.

The entrance is barred by a gilded gate which gave the cathedral the name of Our Saviour behind the Golden Gate. Legend has it that the gate was cast from copper coins minted in the reign of Tsar Alexei to replace silver ones and then taken out of circulation in 1666 following the bloody "copper revolt". In actual fact, however, the gate is wrought from iron which has been painted and gilded. The subtle and intricate beauty of its design is immensely impressive; spiral creepers intertwine with grotesque masks, fantastic beasts and birds and exotic leaves. The Golden Gate is a brilliant example of late seventeenth-century Russian applied art.

The interior of the Cathedral of Our Saviour is cosy and intimate, which is in some measure due to the old tiled stoves placed against the west wall of the refectory and at the altar. There is a four-tiered iconostasis in the main section; the lowest tier contains two icons by Fiodor Zubov, *Longinus the Centurion* and *Theodore Stratelates,* whose interplay of light and shade is characteristic of seventeenth-century icon-painting. The iconostasis itself dates from the mid-eighteenth century and is carved and gilded in the Baroque style. In 1778 two-tiered silver panels with chased reliefs were inserted into the central part of the iconostasis.

The oil-paintings on the walls of the cathedral are of nineteenth-century date. In 1949–52 some seventeenth-century murals were uncovered underneath the later layers in several parts of the vault, but these earlier murals have unfortunately survived only in fragments and are not yet completely cleaned.

The Church of the Crucifixion was built on top of the Cathedral of Our Saviour in 1681, during the reign of Tsar Fiodor. Its famous iconostasis contains extremely unusual icons in which the countenances and hands of the saints are painted in, while the rest of the picture is done in exquisite silk appliqué, carefully colour-matched. These unique pieces were painted in 1682–83 by the Armoury artists Ivan Bezmin, Vasily Poznansky and Bogdan Saltanov. Legend has it that the tsar's daughters did the sewing and appliqué, but in actual fact it was done by the tsarina's seamstresses.

The Church of the Resurrection Glorified stands on the site of the Church of St Eudoxia. Built in 1627, St Eudoxia's was reconstructed and renamed in 1681 in honour of the dedication of the Church of the Resurrection in Jerusalem. At the same time, it was joined to the Church of the Crucifixion on the level of the choir. The focal point of the Church of the Resurrection Glorified is the carved wooden iconostasis, gilded and silvered, dating from the late seventeenth or early eighteenth century. It is especially noteworthy for its lavish architectural forms and decor — jutting cornices, openwork colonnettes formed of curling vines, various cartouches, and luxuriant acanthus leaves. The icons, most of which were painted by Pospelov, date from the same period. A gilded silver chandelier with many holders, which formerly incorporated a clock in its large lower sphere, is a gift to Tsar Alexei from Karl XI, King of Sweden, presented in 1674. The chandelier is in complete harmony with the opulent interior of the church.

The Cathedral of Our Saviour, the Church of the Crucifixion and the Church of the Resurrection Glorified were combined into one complex by Osip Startsev in 1681, when a new roof was built over all three structures. Eleven gilded cupolas were placed on top of the roof, and their barrels were inlaid with shimmering bluish-green majolica. The cornice was embellished with a coloured tiled frieze and the cupolas surmounted with openwork crosses. The tiles and the crosses were designed by the monk Hyppolite, one of the outstanding carver of his time.

The expressive simplicity of the fourteenth- to sixteenth-century structures, the variety and sumptuous decor of the seventeenth-century buildings, and the ingenious architectural forms and decoration of the nineteenth century have made the Great Kremlin Palace an important monument of Russian history and culture, an embodiment of the talent and inventiveness of Russian architects and craftsmen.

The significance of the Great Kremlin Palace was immediately recognized by the Soviet government. A document signed by Anatoly Lunacharsky, People's Commissar of Education, read as follows: "All the buildings and historical monuments within the Kremlin, no matter which authority or institution now runs them, including churches, cathedrals and monasteries, constitute the property of the state." From the very first days of Soviet power the ancient Kremlin was in the thick of the socialist cultural revolution. Two rooms on the lower floor of the building for the Gentlemen in Attendance housed the Moscow Commission for the Preservation of Historical Monuments. One of its former members, the outstanding Soviet sculptor Sergei Konionkov, later recalled: "The Commission realized that the artistic and historical treasures of the ancient capital were of eternal value and, as the property of the nation, should be preserved by all possible means."

Despite severe economic hardships, the Council of People's Commissars, led by Lenin, set aside funds for the restoration of the Kremlin. In January, 1918, 450,000 roubles were allocated for this purpose.

In March 1918, the Soviet government moved from Petrograd to Moscow, and soon afterwards Lenin, concerned about the state of the Kremlin buildings, took the time to inspect them. In May, 1918, he requested that repair work on damaged structures should be speeded up. Research and restoration has subsequently returned to their original state many buildings which had been distorted by later additions and refurbishment.

In 1919 a fragment of the ancient cornice on the east façade of the Tsarina's Golden Chamber was discovered. Subtly and exquisitely decorated with Ionic designs and carved beads, it is yet another convincing example of how the forms of Renaissance architecture were used in the old Kremlin Palace. In 1925 a search for fourteenth-century buildings in the Kremlin resulted in the virtual rediscovery of the Church of the Raising of Lazarus by the architect D. Sukhov and the art historian Nikolai Pomerantsev. The restorers removed the later plasterwork and laid bare the white stone walls. They also uncovered the blocked entrances to the inner staircases, the ancient window apertures, and the round windows whose ribs make them resemble beautiful fan-shaped sea-shells. The original appearance was restored to the west entrance with its typical fourteenth-century portal, and a number of details peculiar to the architectural decor of this remarkable church were revealed.

In 1929 an ancient ornamental fresco was found in the Pantry of the Terem Palace, and the room was completely repainted according to its design. From the late 1940s onwards extensive restoration work was carried out in the Great Kremlin Palace: in 1947 another fragment of a mural was found in the Tsarina's Golden Chamber; in 1949 the wall paintings in the Faceted Palace and the Holy Antechamber were cleaned and reinforced; and in 1950–51 the pictures in the Terem Palace were similarly reworked. In 1952 a test cleaning of the Golden Porch removed the nineteenth-century oil-paintings and exposed the light-coloured seventeenth-century murals. At the same time some fragments of frescoes dating from 1670 in the Cathedral of Our Saviour were stripped of later paint layers.

The next stage of restoration, the largest ever in scope and variety, started in the late 1960s and is still going on. The experts have focused their attention on buildings of all periods. In the nineteenth-century rooms, dilapidated old structures have been replaced and reinforced, the mouldings and gilding have been refurbished, and the marble has been repolished. In addition, the parquet floors have been relaid and the damaged carving on the doors has been repaired. Heavy patterned material and satin woven with silver and gold threads have been specially ordered for the palace and are faithful copies of the original samples in colour and design.

The Great Kremlin Palace has been largely restored to its original splendour. Carefully preserved by the Soviet state, it delights the thousands of visitors who come here to learn about the past and present of this remarkable palace museum, one of the magnificent landmarks in the Moscow Kremlin.

THE ARCHITECTURAL
COMPLEX
OF THE GREAT
PALACE

The Great Kremlin Palace is an integral architectural complex which has evolved over the centuries. It derives its present-day name from that of the palace built in 1849 to the design of Konstantin Thon. The complex incorporates various buildings surviving from previous centuries: the Faceted Palace, the Tsarina's Golden Chamber, and also the Terem Palace and its churches, which had formed part of the old Great Sovereign's Palace of the fifteenth and sixteenth centuries.

One of the best views of the Great Kremlin Palace is from the Great Stone Bridge over the Moscow River. This nineteenth-century complex harmonizes beautifully with the older buildings of the Kremlin, and is the focal point on the Moscow River.

Compositionally, it balances the architectural structures of the ancient Cathedral Square united by the lofty Belfry of Ivan the Great in the centre of the Kremlin. Viewed from the river, the nineteenth-century complex is conceived as a compact group of buildings stretching westward from Cathedral Square to the Borovitsky Tower. The passageway linked the tsar's palace with the Wing of the Grand Princes. Adjoining the latter is the Armoury, built between 1844 and 1851.

5

4. *View of the west façade of the Great Kremlin Palace and of the railing between the Palace and the Armoury*

An iron railing, wrought in the neo-Gothic style popular in Russia during the reign of Nicholas I, divides the main section of the palace from the Armoury. Behind the railing is a small square (formerly Imperial Square), which is now planted with trees and looks entirely different.

5. *The Great Kremlin Palace. Passageway leading from the main section into the Grand Princes' Wing (the former Winter Garden)*

In placing the Winter Garden along the arched passageway leading from the western block of the palace into the Wing of the Grand Princes, Thon followed one of the ancient traditions of Kremlin architecture: he cut transverse arches through the basement, then laid out "hanging" and indoor gardens along the vaults of the arches. One such garden was set out in 1685 in the residence of the thirteen-year-old Peter the Great. The floor of the Winter Garden was laid with lead plates covered with a layer of earth one metre thick and planted with trees, shrubs and flowers. The garden was fenced in by a painted railing with bannisters. Among its attractions were a small pond and a variety of birds, including canaries, parrots and nightingales.

In the nineteenth century, the Winter Garden abounded with plants specially grown in greenhouses, and was adorned with marble statues of Vesta and Hercules, which were later transferred to the Private Apartments.

6. *The Great Kremlin Palace. West façade*

7. *The Great Kremlin Palace. South façade*

The architecture of the Great Kremlin Palace vividly reflects various features characteristic of Russian building techniques in the mid-nineteenth century, primarily the tendency to monumentalize a building by augmenting its absolute dimensions. The main façade is 125 metres long and 44 metres high, and contains about 700 individual rooms and halls with a total area of about 20,000 square metres. A tetrahedral attic topped with a figured cupola towers above the central part of the palace. On the side of the main façade it features ogee archivolts with the moulded state emblem of the Soviet Union and the inscription *USSR* (in place of the former double-headed eagles). A chiming clock was installed in the attic cupola by the brothers Butenop. There is a parapet with bannisters at the base of the attic roof, and a flagstaff in the centre. A gilded railing with two lightning arresters on each side extends along the crest of the roof.

Another distinguishing feature of the palace is its orientation towards Russian architecture of previous centuries rather than towards Classicism. The arcade motif used by Thon in the composition of the first floor was characteristic of the Palace of the Grand Princes of Moscow (it was built in the fifteenth and early sixteenth centuries and stood on this site until the eighteenth century). The upper tiers of the Terem Palace served as a model for the second floor of the new palace, and the exterior decor was borrowed from seventeenth-century structures in the Kremlin.

The walls of the palace are of brick; its pediment is faced with grey stone from a quarry near the village of Tatarov not far from

9

Moscow. The cornices and window surrounds are of white limestone, which has long been quarried near the village of Miachkovo in the Moscow region.

Due to the absence of elements from any of the classical orders, the façade looks flat and its decoration resembles appliqué work. The main entrance is located somewhat east of centre and, incorporated into the rhythmic array of apertures on the front façade, it does not immediately leap to the eye.

9. *The Great Kremlin Palace. Windows on the east façade*

The main feature of the palace's exterior decor is its unusual window apertures. The windows are framed by white limestone surrounds with double arches and pendants. The carved ornamentation was skilfully executed by stone-masons from Santino Campioni's workshop in Moscow. The predominantly plant patterns incorporate figures of heraldic beasts.

10. *View of the east façade of the Great Kremlin Palace and the Faceted Palace from Cathedral Square*

11, 12. *The Faceted Palace*

A significant part of the east façade of the Great Kremlin Palace is hidden by the structures adjoining it. These are the Cathedral of the Annunciation (1485–1489), the former house-chapel of the grand princes and tsars of Moscow, the annex built in the early 1930s, and the Faceted Palace erected between 1487 and 1491 by the architects Marco Ruffo and Pietro Antonio Solari. Its main, east façade, laid with faceted white stone, overlooks Cathedral Square. The palace had a main staircase on the outside and a spacious entrance-hall and large re-ception room inside. Its architecture is a natural blend of Russian and Italian artistic traditions. The very word "palata" derives from the Italian "palazzo", signifying a new type of secular building which evolved in Italy during the Renaissance.

The exterior aspect of the Faceted Palace changed markedly when the original shape and dimensions of the windows were altered, and in particular when they were framed by new carved white limestone surrounds in the late seventeenth century. After this remodelling, the façades became more expressive and decorative, taking on an appearance more in tune with the times.

13. *View of the east façade of the Tsarina's Golden Chamber, the Church of the Deposition of the Robe, and the cupolas of the churches in the Terem Palace from Cathedral Square*

The decor of the old churches integrated into the Great Palace complex lends it an incomparably festive quality. In 1681 the Cathedral of Our Saviour was united with the Church of the Crucifixion and the Church of the Resurrection Glorified by means of a roof and magnificently redecorated on the exterior with a majolica frieze and eleven onion cupolas on tall necks. These brick necks, set on white limestone bases, were adorned with coloured reliefs in Dutch tile. The use of multicoloured enamel tiles for the decoration of the churches in the tsar's residence testified to the fact that a new form of applied art, developed in Moscow during the second half of the seventeenth century by gifted Byelorussian craftsmen, was gaining wide recognition. It is assumed that the well-known tilers Ignat Maximov and Stepan Ivanov worked on the majolica ornamentation of the Terem Palace.

14. *Church of the Deposition of the Robe*

The only façade of the Tsarina's Golden Chamber still unobscured is visible in the depths of Cathedral Square, on its west side. To the left of it is the Faceted Palace, and to the right, the elegant single-domed Church of the Deposition of the Robe. Constructed in the 1480s, this was the main house-chapel in the Metropolitan's Courtyard, which in the fifteenth century occupied the northwest corner of the central Kremlin Square. In the opinion of modern researchers, the Tsarina's Golden Chamber, the reception hall of the tsarina, was built on the site of the Great Metropolitan's Palace by order of Tsar Fiodor in the late sixteenth century.

The façade of the chamber is always enveloped in the shadows cast by the buildings nearby. Its Renaissance cornice, decorated with Ionic designs and beads, is almost entirely concealed. The exterior of the chamber underwent great changes in the seventeenth century.

15. *The Terem Palace. South façade*

The Terem Palace, one of the most interesting buildings in the Moscow Kremlin, is a rare example of secular architecture in the first half of the seventeenth century, which has survived to the present day. Built in 1635–36 by the architects Antip Konstantinov, Trephil Sharutin, Bazhen Ogurtsov, and Larion Ushakov, the palace is remarkable for its harmonious volumes, nobly balanced proportions, expressive silhouette, variously textured walls, and lavishly decorated façades. It is a marvellous piece of architecture, striking in its artistic unity and national flavour. Certain salient features of the architectural decor command attention: the elaborate cornices of ceramic tile on the two upper tiers; the combination of different materials such as fashioned brick, coloured tile and carved white limestone; and the gilded and painted exterior. Almost every year the paint and gilt on the façades were renewed and touched up, and the carving reworked and expanded. According to an account of one of the early stages in this work, in 1673 the gilder Ivan Osipov decorated the roof with ornamental rosettes in silver, gold and various paints, and put mica frames in all the windows of the building.

16

16. *The Terem Palace. Windows on the south façade*

After a fire in 1682, the Terem Palace, along with the entire Great Sovereign's Palace, was refurbished under the supervision of Prince Vasily Golitsyn, a prominent statesman and a well-known patron of the arts. It was at this time that the carved decor of the Terem Palace took its final shape, amalgamating traditional Russian motifs and Western and Oriental designs reworked in the Russian fashion. The carvings embrace a whole world of fancifully interwoven patterns and figures: fantastic multipetalled flowers atop curved stems scattered among parrots, pelicans, imaginary beasts such as gryphons, double-headed eagles, sirens, unicorns, and bushy-tailed lions, mythological cupids, winged trytons, and also falcons pouncing on a bird (falconry is known to have been one of the favourite pastimes of the Russian tsars in the seventeenth century). The Upper Teremok (Attic) and the lower storeys of the Terem Palace are now painted on the outside in a reddish-coral colour, against which the white limestone decor, stripped of its later paint, stands out boldly; the pilasters, the carved window surrounds and the ledges of the upper parapet are dazzlingly white. The original colouring of the exterior, a blend of red brick and white limestone, has been recreated by modern restorers.

17. *View of the north façade of the Terem Palace and the cupolas of its churches from the Palace of Congresses*

19

18. *The Terem Palace. West portal in the Upper Teremok (Attic)*

Much attention was devoted to the portals of the Terem Palace, which have fancifully shaped apertures and rich decor done in white limestone. Popular Russian grasses, heraldic motifs, birds, beasts, masks, and human figures are executed at places in pure white, at others in a bright lacework of multicoloured patterns.

19. *The Terem Palace. Watch-tower*

20. *The Terem Palace. East portal in the Upper Teremok (Attic). Detail*

The east portal of the Teremok is decorated splendidly and lavishly. Above it, there is a carved rectangular panel depicting a mythical creature, exotic birds, squirrels, flowers, and young boys shooting arrows. At the centre of the top of the portal is a popular medieval symbol of Christ's sacrificial death — a bird tearing flesh out of its chest to feed its young. The juxta-position of the fantastic, the humorous and the moral was intended for the tsar's sons, whose room this was. The inscription in Slavic letters over the eastern entrance reads: "By God's grace and the order of the Sovereign, Tsar and Grand Prince Mikhail Fiodorovich, ruler of all Russia, possessor of many kingdoms, these chambers were built for the royal children, Tsarevich Alexei Mikhailovich and Tsarevich Ivan Mikhailovich in the year 7144 from the creation of the world."

THE STATE HALLS
THE CONFERENCE
HALL
OF THE SUPREME
SOVIET
OF THE USSR

While the general composition
of the Great Kremlin Palace
and its exterior decor contain
elements characteristic of the
architecture of bygone centuries,
the interiors exhibit no such ob-
vious parallels with old Russian
art. The dimensions, proportions
and architectural elements of
the rooms conform to the prin-
ciples of Neo-Classicism, with
its passion for regularity and
symmetry. This is particularly
evident in the St George,
St Vladimir and St Catherine
Halls, and also in the decor
of the Conference Hall of the
Supreme Soviet, which tends
towards classical simplicity
and clarity.

21. *The State Vestibule*

Sixteen steps lead from the main entrance of the palace to the State Vestibule, earlier known as the State Antechamber. The flat vaults of this spacious room are supported by four monolithic columns of grey Serdobol granite about eight metres high. Eight pilasters made of the same granite, with veins of lighter colour, are set in the walls. The Doric columns and pilasters have bases and capitals of white Carrera marble. The walls and vaults are faced with imitation marble; soft glow emanating from its surface gives more light to the room.

In the evening, light is provided by four massive, dark brown bronze standard lamps, manufactured in the nineteenth century at the Krumbügel Factory in Moscow. Their entire surface is covered with plant sprays, and the lamp-stands are embellished with tiny facets.

23

22. *The Main Staircase*

The Main Staircase leads from the vestibule to the second floor. Its five flights contain fifty-eight steps and five landings built of Revel stone. A smaller staircase runs down from the third landing to the Annunciation Entrance, which leads to Cathedral Square. The walls of the Main Staircase are faced with yellow imitation marble, polished to a dazzling shine, as are the ten slim pylons with high lancet vaults. Intricately wrought ormolu railings extend between the

pylons, enclosing the galleries along the sides of the staircase. During the Soviet period, the Main Staircase has become known as the Staircase of Honour. In 1961 the world's first cosmonaut, Yuri Gagarin, mounted these stairs amid the festive achromatic of chandeliers, the glare of floodlights, and the sound of triumphal music. All his "brother cosmonauts" later followed in his footsteps, and also the first woman cosmonaut, Valentina Tereshkova. The Main Staircase is also used by the deputies of the Supreme Soviet of the USSR.

23. *The Main Staircase. Crystal vase on the landing outside the Anteroom*

The crystal vase which stands at the entrance to the Anteroom is one of four identical vases decorating the galleries along the sides of the Main Staircase. Such vases were made at the Imperial Glass Factory in St Petersburg from the 1820s onwards. During the 1830s and 40s, the man responsible for designing most of these vases in the Medici style was I. Ivanov, the factory "inventor, draughtsman and titular councillor".

24, 25. *The gallery on the Main Staircase. The Battle of Kulikovo by Adolphe Yvon*

In the right-hand gallery above the Main Staircase hangs a large picture on a subject from Russian history. It is the scene of a fierce battle between the Russian host and Tatar forces in 1380, the famous Battle of Kulikovo. Dmitry Donskoi, the Russian commander, mounted on a rearing horse, his red mantle streaming in the wind, dominates the centre of the canvas. Next to him are Peresvet and Osliabia, two Russian warrior-monks whose names and deeds have come down from old Russian manuscripts.

The Battle of Kulikovo was painted by Adolphe Yvon, a French history and battle painter who was a pupil of the renowned artist Paul Delaroche. Yvon lived in Russia from 1843 to 1845, studying museum collections and Russian everyday life. The canvas, commissioned by Nicholas I, was completed in 1850. Its style echoes that of academic paint-

ing in the first half of the nineteenth century: an atmosphere of allegory and solemnity is combined with a striving for verisimilitude and minute attention to ethnographical detail. This is evident in the rendition of the warriors' armour, faithfully copied from the exhibits Yvon had studied in the oldest Russian museum, the Armoury.

26. *The Anteroom*

The Anteroom is small, covering an area of about 140 square metres, and almost square in plan. The turquoise blue walls are relieved against the starkly white moulding on the vaults, the jasper fireplace, faced with intensely bright variegated stone, and the coloured mosaic of the parquet, inlaid with oak, lemonwood and mahogany.

A wooden tablet set into the edge of the floor informs us that the parquet was made in 1845 at Georg Miller's factory in Moscow.

The focal point of the Anteroom is the painting on the wall opposite the entrance: *Lenin Addressing the Third Congress of the Komsomol*, executed in 1950 by a group of artists headed by B. Ioganson.

27. *The Anteroom.* Lenin Addressing the Third Congress of the Komsomol *by B. Ioganson, V. Sokolov, D. Teghin, N. Faidysh-Krandievskaya, and N. Chebakov. Detail*

28. *The Conference Hall of the Supreme Soviet of the USSR*

The Conference Hall is designed in the form of an elongated rectangle 78 metres long and 20 metres wide. The light colour of the walls creates the illusion of greater space. The double row of windows with arched embrasures in the lower tier face south, on to the Moscow River. On the opposite side of the room there are diplomatic boxes, also arranged in two tiers inside similarly spaced arches; the doors leading to the lobby; and the service rooms, equipped at the same time as the hall. Built in 1932–34, the hall is integrated with the older rooms in the palace: the entrance to the State Apartments is at the front, to the right of the seats for the Praesidium, and the door leading to the St George Hall is at the back behind the last row of seats. The architectural decor of the hall is marked by austerity and economy. Pilasters with Corinthian capitals are set into the walls, a wide cornice extends across the upper part of the room, and the ceiling is smooth and divided up into caissons. The electric lights installed along the cornice are directed upwards and give out a soft, diffused light, and the caissons on the ceiling are adapted for air conditioning.

29. *The Conference Hall of the Supreme Soviet of the USSR. Statue of Lenin by Sergei Merkurov*

A marble statue of Lenin, the founder of the Soviet state, was installed in the Conference Hall in 1939. In a simple and succinct manner the sculptor Sergei Merkurov conveys an image of great inner strength and psychological depth. He reveals the integrity and spiritual force of Lenin's character, his indomitability as a fighter, his wisdom as a thinker, and his simplicity and greatness as a man.

The St George Hall is one of the
most majestic in the Great Kremlin
Palace. Its sumptuous stuccowork is
amazingly rich and intricate. The cylindrical coffered vault is decorated
with curling acanthus leaves and
large rosettes. Luxuriant creepers
intertwined with carved pinnate
leaves abound on the walls and
pylons and above the marble
plaques with gold inscriptions in the
niches. The south and north end
walls have ornamental mouldings
incorporating two identical high reliefs of St George the Victorious,
sculpted by Piotr Klodt.
The dazzling whiteness of the hall
is offset by the ormolu lamps and
stars of the order, the polychrome
squares of carpet and the silk
upholstery of the furniture.
The St George Hall contains the
most beautiful ormolu chandeliers in
the palace. Their openwork design
ensures that they are neither cum-
bersome nor over-elaborate, despite
their large diameter and four-tier
construction. The enormous space
of the room is evenly illuminated by
six chandeliers, which were custom-
made to include the St George
Cross in their decoration.
Until the end of the nineteenth
century candles and oil and kero-
sene lamps were used to light the
palace. Up to 10,000 candles and
5,000 lamps were required just to
illuminate the state rooms on the
second floor. Since 1896 all the
lights in the palace have been fitted
with electric bulbs; 3,000 bulbs are
used for the St George Hall alone.

32. *The St George Hall.*
Southwestern section

Fireplaces as minor architectural
forms play a prominent role in the
organization of space and the decoration of the palace. Fashioned in
various shapes and crafted of rare
decorative stone, the fireplaces are
works of art in their own right.
The white Carrera marble fireplaces
in the St George Hall were manufactured at Santino Campioni's
Moscow workshop. The mantel-
pieces above them are adorned by
bronze sculptural groups and clocks,
produced in St Petersburg by the
firm of Nickols and Plinke after

models by A. Loganovsky. The
sculptural groups are devoted to
heroic and patriotic themes.

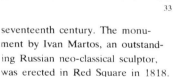

33. *The St George Hall. Clock*
with the sculptural group of Kozma
Minin and Dmitry Pozharsky

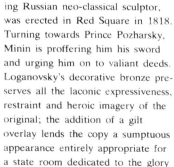

A clock decorated with the sculptural group of Kozma Minin and
Dmitry Pozharsky stands on the
mantelpiece above the fireplace in
the eastern part of the St George
Hall. The sculpture is a reduced
copy of the famous monument to
Minin and Pozharsky, who were
heroes of the popular resistance to
foreign invaders in the early

seventeenth century. The monument by Ivan Martos, an outstanding Russian neo-classical sculptor,
was erected in Red Square in 1818.
Turning towards Prince Pozharsky,
Minin is proffering him his sword
and urging him on to valiant deeds.
Loganovsky's decorative bronze pre-
serves all the laconic expressiveness,
restraint and heroic imagery of the
original; the addition of a gilt
overlay lends the copy a sumptuous
appearance entirely appropriate for
a state room dedicated to the glory
of Russian arms.

34

34. *The St George Hall. Southern section*

The few pieces of furniture in the St George Hall are restrained in form. The low benches and stools have twisted gilt legs and seats upholstered in rep the same colour as the ribbons of the order.
Two identical ormolu caskets, decorated with plant relief patterns and emblems of the order, stand on tall white marble pedestals by the windows in the southern part of the hall. The front of each one is deco-

rated with an enamel Cross of St George encircled by a ribbon of the order inscribed with the device *For service and bravery*. The caskets, crafted by the Moscow bronze-worker Poltavtsev, contain manuscript lists of all those who received the Order of St George the Victorious from 1769, when Catherine II founded the order, to 1885. The names on this list are also engraved in gold on the marble plaques.

35. *The St George Hall. Statue of Little Russia by Ivan Vitali*

The *Little Russia* sculpture in the St George Hall, a symbol of the voluntary union of the Ukraine and Russia in 1654, was executed in marble by Ivan Vitali in Moscow in 1845–49. It stands by the pylon on the right-hand side of the hall, in front of the entrance to the Conference Hall of the Supreme Soviet. Eight other statues also tower above the columns and the cornice on the same side.

36, 37. *The St George Hall.*
Parquet floor

Many Russian palaces and country
estates are famous for their inlaid
parquet floors. The most outstanding examples of this original art
date from the eighteenth and early
nineteenth centuries. In the St
George Hall, the wooden floor is
"carpeted" in a striking combination
of colours. Crafted after a sketch by
F. Solntsev, it is notable for its
superb workmanship. Solntsev was
attracted to old Russian art and,
in particular, to book illumination,
which probably accounts for the
somewhat fanciful combinations
in his decorative compositions.
The design of the floor is rich and
varied, including both geometrical
and plant motifs. The main ground
consists of a neutral geometrical
pattern accentuated in the middle
by a triangular frieze; in the centre
is an intricate rosette enclosed in a
rhombus. Numerous details in valuable species of wood are inlaid into
the parquet, creating a panel in a
colourful blend of contrasting tones,
from lemon-yellow to violet and
from greenish-grey to red. The overall colour scheme of the floor is
golden, since its main part is made
up of light beechwood.

38. *The St Vladimir Hall. Southern
section*

39. *The St Vladimir Hall. Western
section*

The architectural decor of the
St Vladimir Hall is dominated by
arches. These are supplemented by
columns, semi-columns, pilasters,
cornices, profiled bands, and ornamental hollows. The composition
includes the windows and portals of
the Tsarina's Golden Chamber and
Zhiletskaya Chamber, which face
into the St Vladimir Hall and are visible through the wide lower arches
on its north side. The coloured
imitation marble and the abundance
of stucco moulding and gilt create
an impression of grandeur.
A staircase leads up from the
western section of the hall to the
upper gallery. The bannisters are
supported by an ormolu trellis
thickly patterned with spiralling
stems and sprays of flowers.
In design, this trellis matches the
plant mouldings in the hall.

41

40, 41. *The St Vladimir Hall. Vault with stucco mouldings*

Two experts in plasterwork, the serf brothers Fiodor and Nikolai Dylev, were responsible for the beautiful mouldings in the Great Kremlin Palace. These skilled artisans crafted whimsical scrolls, flowers and leaves on the vault of the St Vladimir Hall. The repetitive pattern covers all sixteen sails of the vault. Crosses and stars of the Order of St Vladimir, encircled by garlands of oak-leaves, alternate in the centre of the ornament. The bases of the dividing bands are adorned with

double-headed eagles which, like all the mouldings in the hall, are covered with a layer of gilt.

42. *The St Vladimir Hall. Staircase leading to the gallery and the Terem Palace*

The banquettes in the St Vladimir Hall are upholstered in red and black silk, the colours of the ribbons of the order. Tall ormolu candelabra on red marble supports stand in the niches at the corners of the room. The parquet floor is almost entirely composed of geometrical motifs; its expressive design is

effectively accentuated by insets of black fumed oak which contrast sharply with the light walnut and oak ground. The small gilded tables with bentwood legs are usually brought into the hall for ceremonies involving the signing of government acts or the awarding of state honours.

43. *The Winter Garden. Fountain and niche inlaid with mosaic*

The Winter Garden was planted on the site of the former Boyar Gathering-place, on the west side of the St Vladimir Hall, in 1959. Designed by S. Andreyev, G. Wolfson, V. Dolganov, M. Prokhorov, and E. Krupnova, it is rectangular in shape, its floor and walls laid with plates of various kinds of Caucasian marble. One wall is entirely glazed in and the opposite is set with a wide mirror, which creates an illusion of even more space. High up on the end walls, above the greenery, there are air vents covered by wrought openwork gratings with designs based on Russian folk motifs. The mosaic goldfish pond is sprinkled by a pyramid-shaped fountain made of large varicoloured glass crystals. In this setting, suffused with light and filled with the gurgling of running water, stands *Fallow Deer*, a statue cast in metal in the hollow relief technique. The graceful animals are delineated only in contour; silhouetted sharply against the wall and framing the lively back-and-forth motion of the leaves, they seem at one with their environment. The piece was sculpted by I. Yefimov, the master who introduced the hollow relief technique into decorative sculpture. The very concept of hollow relief goes back to the old Russian tradition of cast and wrought railings, of which there are several excellent examples in the Great Kremlin Palace.

THE STATE
APARTMENTS

The state rooms in the west wing of the Great Kremlin Palace are known as the State, or Catherine, Apartments. They form a regular suite with all the doors on one axis. The large mirror at the end of the suite creates an illusion of an endless series of rooms extending into the distance.

This part of the palace owes its second name to the hall once dedicated to the Order of St Catherine, which was bestowed only on women. The St Catherine Hall was formerly the throne room of the Russian empresses.

44. *The Chevalier Guard's Room in the State Apartments*

The south end wall of the Chevalier Guard's Room adjoins the section of the Conference Hall which up to 1932 was the St Andrew Hall. The door in the north end wall leads to the St Catherine Hall and the suite of State Apartments.

The functional purpose of this room in the past (a picket of Chevalier Guards was stationed here) accounts for its modest appearance when compared to some of the other State Apartments. The monotonous white of the walls, stuccoed to imitate marble, is broken only by the bright patches of ormolu on the chandelier, candelabra, fireplace, and clocks. The geometrically patterned parquet floor is inlaid in walnut, beech and mahogany, enlivened by insets of valuable light-coloured species.

45. *The Chevalier Guard's Room in the State Apartments. Bronze candelabrum*

Bronze *objets d'art* reappear over and over again in the Great Kremlin Palace, especially in the state halls. Numerous and varied lighting fixtures such as chandeliers, candelabra and candlesticks are fashioned of bronze. The large ten-branched candelabra in the Chevalier Guard's Room are remarkable for their half-length figures of angels bearing candlesticks.

46

46. *The Chevalier Guard's Room
in the State Apartments. Clock and
vases on the mantelpiece*

Most of the items of decorative art
in the Great Kremlin Palace are the
work of Russian craftsmen, but
there is also a small yet interesting
collection of mantelpiece ornaments
by French bronze-workers. The late
eighteenth- and early nineteenth-
century French clocks in the first-
floor rooms and a few in the State
Apartments charm the viewer with
their variety of shape and decoration. Among them is the bronze

clock on the mantelpiece of the
Chevalier Guard's Room.
Probably produced in the mid-
nineteenth century, it is known as
Raphael in the Temple of Glory.
The seated figure of the great
master is framed by an arch above
which is the clock face. Besides the
clock, two French vases of the same
period adorn the mantelpiece. Their
vigorous silhouettes, embellished by
sculpted *putti* riding hippocampi,
contrast with the balanced architectural form of the clock case.

The decor of the St Catherine Hall,
the main State Apartment, combines
sumptuousness with impeccable taste.
The six crystal candelabra in the
hall are truly out of the ordinary.
Beautifully designed and elegantly
mounted in ormolu, they look like
the crowns of fantastic trees. The
candelabra were made at the Imperial Glass Factory in St Petersburg,
where remarkably fine monumental
works famous not only in Russia
but also abroad were produced.
Each candelabrum is 4.5 metres
high and mounted on a base of red
French marble with white veins,
which blends well with the other
colours in the hall. The silhouettes
of the candelabra stand out
prominently against the walls, covered in silvery moire with borders
formed of the pinkish-red ribbons
of St Catherine's Order. The bows
at the top of the walls are also tied
from ribbons of the order, strewn
with large artificial diamonds and
massive emblems with the device of
the order.

48. *The St Catherine Hall.*
Furniture in the eastern section

This state hall was not planned to
include any furniture, except the
Empress' throne. Now the
nineteenth-century throne with its
unwieldy canopy has been removed.
In its place there are straight chairs,
armchairs and sofas in white and
gilt, taken from drawing-room sets
in the style of Late Russian Classicism, and also small round tables
with mirror tops and elaborately
ornamented legs in the Second
Rococo style.

49. *The St Catherine Hall.*
Northern section

The parquet floor of this hall, like
all mosaic floors in the Great Kremlin Palace, has undoubted historical value. Assembled in panels, it
is a fine piece of parquetry, bold in
technique and done with exquisite
workmanship in a beautiful assort-
ment of coloured woods. The pattern, designed by F. Solntsev,
is emphatically decorative
and packed with intricate combinations of geometrical and stylized
plant motifs. The basic rhomboid
grid with rosettes of leaves
effectively sets off the oval panels
with cross-shaped flowers and
arabesque scrolls. One such panel
is clearly seen near the door
leading from the hall to the State
Drawing Room.

50. *The St Catherine Hall. Ormolu chandelier*

The chandeliers in the hall were made in 1845–49 at the Felix Chopin factory in St Petersburg. They are examples of the new type of ormolu chandeliers without crystal decoration which came into vogue in Russia during the first half of the nineteenth century. The bronze was gilded by means of the firing technique, which gave it a pleasant even shine. The Chopin factory was the main supplier of ormolu chandeliers to the Great Kremlin Palace.

51. *The St Catherine Hall. Doors*

The doors of the St Catherine Hall are decorated with gilded and silvered reliefs, and a medallion, star and ribbon of the order.

52. *View of the State Drawing Room from the St Catherine Hall*

53. *The State Drawing Room. Eastern section*

The interior decor of the State Apartments is conspicuous for its great richness. The St Catherine Hall, with its pale silvery colour scheme relieved only by touches of gilt on the ribs of the vault, leads into the State Drawing Room. The latter has walls and furniture uphol-stered in greenish-gold brocade, dark rosewood doors, variegated porcelain standard lamps, and bright, colourful ceiling paintings by Giuseppe Colombo Artari. The doors, crafted in rosewood by Blechschmidt, are embellished with large mirrors, inlays of valuable woods, brass and mother-of-pearl, and exquisitely fashioned bronze overlays. They can truly be counted among the numerous art treasures of the Kremlin Palace.

54. *The State Drawing Room. Window and fireplace in the western section*

55. *The State Drawing Room. Furniture and porcelain standard lamps*

The furniture of the State Drawing Room is arranged in groups near the walls. The sofas, armchairs and straight chairs form compact circles around the little tables placed near two niches containing tall, painted six-branch porcelain standard lamps ornamented in bronze. The niches themselves, faced with snow-white marble, not only provide an ideal background for these magnificent lamps, but also reflect and intensify the light which they shed.

Just as all the porcelain for the palace was supplied by the Imperial Porcelain Factory and most of the furniture by the Gambs and Tour factories in St Petersburg, so the material for the upholstery was all produced at the Moscow factory of G. Sapozhnikov, purveyor of goods to the royal court. The textiles made by this firm were considered to be the best in Russia and gained wide recognition abroad following numerous world exhibitions held from 1851 onwards. The Sapozhnikov factory turned out excellent quality damask, velvet and brocade in various shades, including the green-on-gold pattern in brocade and silk used to upholster the walls and furniture of the room.

56. *The State Drawing Room. Painted plafond*

57. *The State Bedchamber. Doors*

Like the parquet floors, the doors
of the state rooms in the Great
Kremlin Palace seem to vie with
one another in beauty and
workmanship. The doors of the
State Bedchamber are made of
rosewood adorned with delicate
inlays and elegant ornamented
plaques of ormolu. They beautifully
match the stately character of the
room and were, like those in the
State Drawing Room, crafted by
Blechschmidt.

58, 59. *The State Bedchamber. Northern section*

The canopied bed is the only item in the State Bedchamber which has not survived to the present time. The sofas, armchairs, large standing mirror, and the crystal standard lamps in the niches occupy their original places. This can be verified from a drawing by K. Ukhtomsky, who sketched the bedchamber in the middle of the nineteenth century. One rare feature of the room is the *Psyche* standing mirror in a gilded, carved wooden frame.

In the decor of the State Bedchamber wide use has been made of natural and artificial marble in various shades: white for the ceiling and the niches; a combination of light green sprinkled with grey and white and pinkish-grey for the cornice skirting the room; and green for the ten pilasters along the walls. The focal points are the two columns of greenish-grey marble, the largest and most valuable monoliths of this rare stone in Russia.

The alcove is partitioned by columns in the eastern half of the room, which contains a large mirror

and several pieces of elegant gilded furniture with quilted upholstery, characteristic of the sets produced at the Gambs factory.

60

60. *The State Bedchamber. Clock and candlesticks on the jasper mantelpiece*

61. *The State Bedchamber. Window and fireplace in the western section*

Fireplaces as minor architectural forms play an important role in the organization and decoration of the interiors of the Great Kremlin Palace.
Beautifully crafted in rare kinds of decorative stone, they are one of the most attractive features of the palace. The jasper fireplace in the State Bedchamber is distinguished by elegant simplicity and severity of line and colour. Made at the Ekaterinburg Lapidary Factory, which was well known as early as the eighteenth century, it is one of the best examples of Russian stone-masonry, an art which had flourished in the Urals for many centuries.

The clock and candelabra installed on the mantelpiece are the work of nineteenth-century French craftsmen. The dynamic plastic shape of the Second Rococo clocks contrasts with the strict, clear-cut lines of the fireplace and the calm, classical nobility of the dark patinated sculptures of the candelabra.

62

62. *The Walnut Cloak Room.*
Alabaster chandelier

63. *The Walnut Cloak Room*

The light walnut panelling of the
Cloak Room walls and ceiling was
executed by the Moscow
craftsman K. Hertz.
The panels fit together perfectly,
without the use of glue.
The two large windows on the west
wall of the Walnut Cloak Room
flood the room with light. At night,
illumination is provided by a chan-

delier skilfully cut from alabaster,
with an elegant plant design on
its sides. Indistinguishable against
the milk-white surface in daylight,
the pattern leaps to the eye when
the lamps are lit. The chandelier
was manufactured in 1845—49,
probably at Santino Campioni's
workshop; its shape shows the influence of classical models,
imitations of which were popular
in court art in the early nineteenth century.
A number of the State Apartments
terminate in the Walnut Cloak

Room. Beyond the end door there
is a small, gently sloping staircase
leading to the White Corridor
formerly used by the Empress'
ladies-in-waiting.
The windows and door of the ancient Church of the Nativity of the
Virgin open into this corridor, which
connects the State Apartments with
the St Vladimir Hall.

64

64. *The White Corridor between the State Apartments and the St Vladimir Hall*

The White Corridor was constructed in 1838–49 on the site of one of the open outdoor passages of the old royal palace, near the ancient terems, or bedchambers. For this reason, it is also known as the Terem Gallery. The corridor is adorned with arched windows which in rhythm and form resemble a traditional arcade. Thon placed the corridor along the second floor of the structures enclosing the inner courtyard on the north side.

THE PRIVATE
APARTMENTS

The Private Apartments of the
Great Kremlin Palace represent
a veritable museum of Russian
palatial decoration, whose appearance has essentially not
changed since the 1840s.
Placed according to a well-
thought-out plan, the various
items in this suite, including the
antique furniture, harmonize
beautifully with the spatial arrangement of the rooms. While
fulfilling a strictly utilitarian
purpose, they are at the same
time true works of decorative
and applied art. The originality
of this interior stems from a
mingling of the traditional and
the new: the rooms, laid out in
a regular suite, show the influence of late Neo-Classicism,
but the rigid stylistic unity
which distinguished the decor
has disappeared. The furniture
and *objets d'art* are set out
in such a way as to create an
air of cosiness and comfort.

66

66. *The Dining Room. Porcelain vase with representation of Kozma Minin and Dmitry Pozharsky*

One of the vases depicts an event which took place at the beginning of the seventeenth century. Kozma Minin and Patriarch Hermogene are exhorting Prince Dmitry Pozharsky to lead the Russian people in their struggle against foreign invaders. This is a subject often encountered in Russian art, one which many sculptors, artists and craftsmen have treated at various times.

65. *The Dining Room. Northern section*

The architecture and decor of the room have retained their original form almost entirely since the mid-nineteenth century. The rather cold tones of the stucco trim made to imitate marble, and the division of the walls into glossy whitish-yellow surfaces remain the dominant features of the room. The perfect smoothness of the plaster is enlivened by the moulded ornamental reliefs which form bands and circles against the snow-white ceiling. The piers and niches contain elegant statues and vases.

Two large porcelain vases catch the eye with their beautiful proportions and classical clarity of form. They are adorned with scenes from seventeenth- and eighteenth-century Russian history. These vases were among the finest articles manufactured at the Imperial Porcelain Factory during the first quarter of the nineteenth century. Both are signed: beneath the painting on one is written *Painted by S. Golov from a sketch by Professor A. Ivanov, 1827*, the other bears the inscription *Painted by V. Meshcheriakov from a sketch by Professor A. Ivanov, 1827*.

*67. The Dining Room. Porcelain
vase with representation of Peter
the Great and Catherine I*

The other vase depicts a scene from
Peter the Great's Prut campaign
against the Turks in 1711, named
after the River Prut, which flows
into the Black Sea. The action takes
place in Peter's tent where, along
with Russian commanders, his wife
Catherine is present. It was because
of her selfless behaviour in the face
of her husband's imminent capture
that the Order of St Catherine was
founded in Russia (one of the state
rooms in the Great Kremlin Palace
is dedicated to this order).

68. *The Dining Room. Pylon with niche*

69. *The Dining Room. Marble vase*

The decor of every private apartment is dominated by one particular type of object. In the Dining Room, where classical and Renaissance motifs reign, marble vases and sculpture play a major role. The themes of the sculptures are taken from Graeco-Roman mythology. Figures of Leda and Hymen are sculpted in the round, the crater vases are embossed with maenads and satyrs in relief on the sides and with Olympic goddesses on the base. Vases with such figures and designs were called *Borghese* in Russia after the famous Borghese collection comprising imitations and copies of genuine Greek and Roman vases.

70. *The Drawing Room. "Corridor" section*

In almost every private apartment there are massive pylons, which support the walls of the upper floor and which account for the unusual layout of these rooms. Starting with the Drawing Room, each apartment is divided into two sections with different dimensions and uses.
The front sections, through which the axis of the suite passes, have windows and a fireplace and are more ceremonial; they function as a kind of corridor which immediately leaps to the visitor's eye. The back or "intimate" sections, hidden in the depths beyond the pylons, were used for household work and relaxation. They are divided either by a screen or by a carved wooden openwork lattice.

71

71. *The Drawing Room.*
Porcelain standard lamp

The porcelain in this room differs greatly from the classical pieces in the Dining Room. In shape, colour scheme and subject matter, the china vases, lamps and clocks in the Drawing Room are deliberate imitations of the *objets d'art* made by French craftsmen for Madame de Pompadour. The pale blue many-branched candelabra mounted in figured ormolu are as ornate as articles fashioned in the Second Rococo and Pompadour styles. Their vase shape, their brilliant turquoise colouring, and their picturesque pastoral scenes and floral designs are all based on the traditions of Sèvres ware during the reign of Louis XV.

72. *The Drawing Room.*
Western section

The Second Rococo style, based on mid-eighteenth century French artistic forms, was widely used in Russian interiors of the 1840s. The decorators did not attempt to copy the original articles slavishly; in fact, they often borrowed only the shape and design. Much effort was expended to create an atmosphere of lavish elegance. In the Drawing Room this effect is produced by the figured silk of the walls windows and soft furniture; the painted and moulded ceilings; the gilt details on the ceilings and vaults; and the numerous mirrors lining the hall. The "intimate" section of the Drawing Room is partitioned off by a carved and gilded wooden lattice.

·73. *The Drawing Room.*
"Intimate" section

The "intimate" section of the
Drawing Room is painted in calm
light colours. The walls and gilded
furniture, smooth and rounded in
shape, are upholstered in white
patterned silk.

Judging by the Rococo elements
present in the furniture — the characteristic curving contours, the
carved tableboards, the profiled
gilded wood, as well as the compact-
ness and massiveness typical of the

style — we can deduce that it was
manufactured at the Gambs
factory during the 1840s.

74. *The Drawing Room.*
Porcelain chandelier

This unique polychrome chandelier
with moulded porcelain flowers is
an excellent example of the fine
workmanship displayed by nineteenth-century Russian ceramic artists, who inherited the art of moulding delicate china flowers from the
outstanding craftsman P. Ivanov.

He worked at the Imperial
Porcelain Factory from 1808
to 1829 and was renowned for his
ingeniously crafted flower compositions in biscuit. Some of the
porcelain bouquets he made are in
the Russian Museum in Leningrad.

75. *The Empress' Study*

The specific layout of the Empress'
Study is determined by two central
pylons (instead of one as in the
other rooms). The interior is thus
subdivided not only into "corridor"
and "intimate" sections, but further
split up into compartments. The
"intimate" section has secluded corners for reading, playing music and
relaxing by the fireside. It is interesting that the Study is the only
private apartment where the fireplace is set far in the depths of the
room rather than opposite, between
the windows of the front section.

76. *The Empress' Study.*
Northwestern section

The furniture and doors of the Empress' Study are inlaid with tortoise-shell and ormolu or brass in the Boulle style. The patterns for these inlays were cut simultaneously from two sheets, one metal and one tortoise-shell, placed one on top of the other. The cut-out designs were then combined to produce either a shell ground inlaid with ormolu or brass, or an ormolu and brass ground inlaid with specially treated shell. This juxtaposition of materials

rendered the ornament particularly effective. As well as being adorned with buhlwork, the sides of the small cupboards and the central part of the doors feature exquisite ebony and walnut *intarsia* panels inset with mother-of-pearl. The opulence of this decoration is intensified by the cast bronze overlays on the furniture and doors.

77. *The Empress' Study.*
Doors. Detail

78. *The Empress' Study.*
Crystal chandelier

The crystal chandeliers hanging in
the Private Apartments lend the
rooms particular elegance; each
room has one of a different design.
Nineteenth-century chandeliers seem
more massive than their eighteenth-
century counterparts; their metal
skeleton is often completely hidden
by crystal embellishment. Those
in the Study were produced in
St Petersburg during the 1840s

and resemble cascades of pendants
shaped like beads and prisms. The
upper parts of the chandeliers are
also made up of pendants. The
bright silver skeleton is completely
obscured by the radiant, iridescent
crystal fringes. The decorative and
lighting effect in the Empress' Study
is considerably enhanced by the
bright shine and refractive capacity
of crystal.

79. *The Empress' Study.*
Marble fireplace

80. *The passageway. Marble vase:*
Three Bacchantes

81. *The passageway between the*
Empress' Study and the Boudoir

The passageways in the Private
Apartments were intended as sitting
rooms for the personal attendants
of the tsar's family. The empress'
attendants, or ladies of the Bedchamber, would await their mistress'
pleasure in the room situated between the Study and the Boudoir;
hence its alternative name, Attendants' Sitting Room.

This room differs from all the
others in the suite in that its walls
are not hung with material but
embellished with painted leaf patterns
àgainst a scarlet background. Abundant wood-carvings cover the panels, columns, cornices, and dark,
evenly painted walnut doors. The
marble vase by the window contrasts effectively with the multicoloured decor of the interior.

In the Boudoir and the Bedroom,
rooms set aside for rest and soli-
tude, an impression of cosiness is
achieved by the carefully thought-
out arrangement of the furniture in
the "intimate" sections. The nature
of the furniture itself is a major
factor. Soft, unbronzed and rounded
in shape, with curved legs and
quilted backs, the Gambs armchairs
and sofas seem natural and right for
their setting. They are characteristic
examples of the so-called
Walnut Rococo.

The allocation of orders between
court purveyors to the Great Kremlin Palace was probably organized in
the same way as during the restoration of the Winter Palace in
St Petersburg after a fire in 1837.
The furniture for Nicholas I's rooms
came from André Tour's factory
and the furniture for his wife's suite
from Peter Gambs' factory. The
archives of the Great Palace
contain plans of the State
Drawing Room and the Bedchamber
in the Private Apartments with a
note written in 1848: "The arrangement of the furniture approved by
the tsar; a model will be supplied
by Gambs."

To the right, in the depths of the
Boudoir, a door opens into the
bathroom, or, as it is called in
nineteenth-century accounts, the
"washroom", which has a marble
bath and an alabaster chandelier.

83

83, 84. *The Boudoir.*
Malachite fireplace

The fireplace in the Boudoir is a
magnificent example of Russian mosaic, composed of pieces of malachite, which is known, not without
reason, as the Russian stone. The
largest deposits of malachite were
discovered in the Urals in 1814.
The craftsmen at the Demidov and
Turchaninovs factories achieved
great mastery in working this stone.
The technique consists in the careful
facing of surfaces with thin plates
of malachite. To attain the desired

effect it is essential to select the
plates according to their colour
and natural pattern, and to create
the impression of an object sculpted
from a single monolith. In Russia,
malachite was customarily used in
combination with ormolu, which
produced an extremely rich colour
spectrum. This traditional combination is also found in the malachite
rooms of the Great Kremlin Palace:
the pilasters in the St Catherine
Hall have ormolu capitals, and the
fireplace in the Boudoir is adorned
with ormolu plaques in the shape of
sirens, cartouches and rosettes.

86

85, 86. *The Bedroom*

Three shades predominate in the colour scheme of the room, namely dark blue, white and gold.

The walls and pylons are hung with deep blue moire, the same material used for the heavy window drapes and the upholstery of the gilded chairs placed near the windows in the "corridor" section.

Judging by their simple, conventional shape, completely at variance with that of the other furniture in the room, they were originally intended for one of the state halls and probably made at André Tour's factory.

Tiny bouquets and dainty floral scrolls adorn the ceiling, which, together with the vaults of the arches, is bordered by gilded ornamental bands. The beauty of the white fireplace of pure, unveined marble is enhanced by a low gilded lattice in a dense filigree pattern and by the traditional clock and candelabra on the mantelpiece.

As in almost all the private rooms, the clock is of French workmanship.

A bronze sculpted group entitled *Night* rests on a low figured plinth with a profiled edge. At the top, two gilded figures of *putti* holding torches curve around the sides of a black sphere inscribed with gold numbers and stars; at the base, there are two recumbent, semi-nude female figures.

87. *The Emperor's Study.*
Vase and candelabra

88. *The Emperor's Study*

The Emperor's Study is a corner
room, the last in the suite of Private Apartments. It resembles an
elongated rectangle in shape and is
open in layout (without pylons).
One of its three windows faces
south and the other two are on the
west façade of the palace, looking
in the direction of the Borovitsky
Gate and the Armoury. The wood
panelling, the leather-upholstered
furniture seen in this room had
been widely used in the studies of
grand Russian homes by the mid-
nineteenth century. The ceiling is
adorned with paintings and mouldings, and a pier-glass is set above
the fireplace, between the windows.
Only small details of the original
decor have been changed: the old

chandelier has been replaced by a
lamp with many bulbs covered by
bell-like shades of frosted glass,
done in the Russian Art Nouveau
style of the late nineteenth and
early twentieth century; and
a large canvas which hung in the
Study for a time, *Ivan the Terrible*
Setting Out on a Pilgrimage by
N. Sverchkov, was transferred to the
Armoury after 1917.

89, 90. *The Emperor's Reception Room. Sofa, and table inlaid with Florentine mosaic*

The most eye-catching feature of the Emperor's Reception Room is its unity of decor. The light-coloured walls, painted to resemble silk, match the floral ceiling decor beautifully. Floral motifs also prevail in the upholstery material, and culminate in the magnificent flower designs on the tabletop in front of the large sofa. At first sight it seems that the bouquet in the centre of the perfectly polished black marble plate is painted against the dark background. In actual fact, the entire design is composed of jasper, agate, nephrite, and lapis lazuli inset in the Florentine mosaic technique (smooth inlays of large laminae of varicoloured decorative and semi-precious stones).

This technique is notable for its use of the natural colours and patterns of stone — patches, veins and shadows, hence another name, "shadow mosaic". Polishing plays an exceptionally important role in the Florentine mosaic process, because it reveals the abundant nuances of colour in the stone. Well known for its Florentine mosaics was the Peterhof Stonecrafting Factory. It was founded in 1725 and flourished a second time during the 1840s and 60s, becoming famous for the skilfully crafted articles it produced for the interiors of the royal palaces and the homes of the élite. In addition to the table already mentioned, one other item from this factory is found in the Empress' Drawing Room — an elegant writing-desk decorated with Florentine mosaic. The sides and drawers of this desk are finished

91

with coloured stones inset
against black marble. The exquisite
garlands of flowers, posies of forget-
me-nots, and altering triangles
and circles of pink, red, blue, dark
blue, white, and brownish-yellow
flowers are formed of various kinds
of jasper, agate, lapis lazuli, and
rhodonite.

91. *The Valets' Room in the
Private Apartments. Crystal pitcher*

Even the most modest rooms in the
Private Apartments, those intended
for servants, contain scores of valuable *objets d'art.*

In the Valets' Room adjoining the
emperor's quarters, there are two
large and very interesting crystal
pitchers. The wide convex sides of
each vessel are cut with wedge-
shaped facets which cover the entire surface of the heavy crystal in a
distinct grid-like pattern. This decoration resembles the faceting of a
precious stone, hence its name
"diamond-cut". Other types of
facets, characteristic of nineteenth-century glassware, are also
used on the pitchers; the bands on
the spherical bodies of the vessels
are "circle-cut" and the cylindrical
necks are "rib-cut".

THE SMALLER
PALACES OF THE
15th AND 16th
CENTURIES

After the Faceted Palace, the Holy Antechamber, the Tsarina's Golden Chamber, and Zhiletskaya Chamber, all palace structures of the fifteenth and sixteenth centuries, were integrated with the Great Kremlin Palace, their interiors formed a harmonious whole with the rooms of the new palace. The unique beauty of the old chambers complemented the grandeur of the nineteenth-century halls.

92. *The Holy Antechamber and the portal of the Faceted Palace from the St Vladimir Hall*

93. *The Holy Antechamber*

The Holy Antechamber was assigned a major role in court ceremonial. It connected the Faceted Palace with the Red Porch and the four stately flights of the Red Stairway, which led down to Cathedral Square. Much attention was devoted to the decoration of the Holy Antechamber and the Red Stairway. In the seventeenth century, the wooden roof covering the stairs was replaced by a copper one and three tent roofs were built above the landings. White stone lions, the work of Grigory Ivanov, were installed on the parapets of the landings. The foot of the staircase was barred by a gate painted to resemble gold. After various fires, the Antechamber and Stairway were renovated and repaired several times. The Stairway was torn down in 1932-34, and a service annex was erected in its place by the south wall of the Faceted Palace. The main access to the Holy Antechamber is now through the doors of the St Vladimir Hall, which open directly on to the tall outer portal of the Faceted Palace with its triangular pediment and abundance of ornamental carvings and gildings. The murals of the Antechamber were executed by Fiodor Zavyalov during the 1840s in the manner of academic historical paintings. Subject compositions adorn the side walls, the semi-circles under the vaults and the end wall opposite the old entrance to the Red Stairway. The lower part of the walls is entirely covered with Late Renaissance motifs.

94. *The Faceted Palace. Inner portal*

The inner portal of the Faceted Palace is ascribed by researchers to a fairly wide period—from the late fifteenth to the seventeenth century. This dating reflects the various stages in the history of the portal. Whereas the shape, articulation and motifs used in the carved decor are characteristic of the stone portals introduced to the Moscow Kremlin by Italian architects at the very beginning of the sixteenth century, the somewhat dry manner of execution is more typical of the latter part of the period and may have resulted from restoration work in the sixteenth and seventeenth centuries. The top of the portal is interesting too: it is crowned in totally Russian fashion by an ogee arch, which was an extremely common device in fifteenth-century Russian architecture. Beneath a curving ornamental band, two snow-leopards hold shields in their paws; between them are a lion mask and a double-headed eagle. The eagle became part of the Muscovite coat-of-arms under Grand Prince Ivan III. Since the Faceted Palace was built by order of Ivan III and served a definite ceremonial purpose, it is easy to imagine how significant the heraldic decorations on the portal were. The motif of the Russian state emblem is repeated in the lower part of the pilasters flanking the portal.

95, 96. *The Faceted Palace. Interior*

Decorated with murals and gilt, the interior of the Faceted Palace is both majestic and striking; its gilded portal and central pier glow with a festive radiance. The walls and vaults are completely covered with bright, multifigure compositions. Light pours into the room through the numerous windows arranged in two tiers. Artificial light is provided by four massive dark bronze chandeliers and twenty smaller ones of the same metal.

The chandeliers for the Faceted Palace were manufactured in the early 1880s at the Felix Chopin factory in St Petersburg. Their design is largely based on fifteenth- and sixteenth-century circular Novgorod *khoroses*. The basic shape of the *khoros* was preserved in the chandeliers, but two upper tiers, smaller in diameter, were added. The openwork representations of winged centaurs found on the lower tiers of *khoroses* were retained, but the medieval interwoven design of the Novgorod pieces was replaced by a more complex ornament incorporating stems and leaves.

The ancient furniture of the palace harmonized in rhythm and form with the interior itself. Benches set on low wooden platforms stood along the walls, the tsar's throne, raised on several steps, was placed near the east wall, between the windows. The furniture of the Faceted Palace and Holy Antechamber now consists of low benches and chairs with high carved backs and twisted legs. Twentieth-century in date, they are modelled on late seventeenth-century palace furniture. From the earliest times, the Faceted Palace was heated by warm air from stoves on the floor below: there were no stoves in the Palace itself. The hot air came through vents covered with gratings on the floor near the west wall.

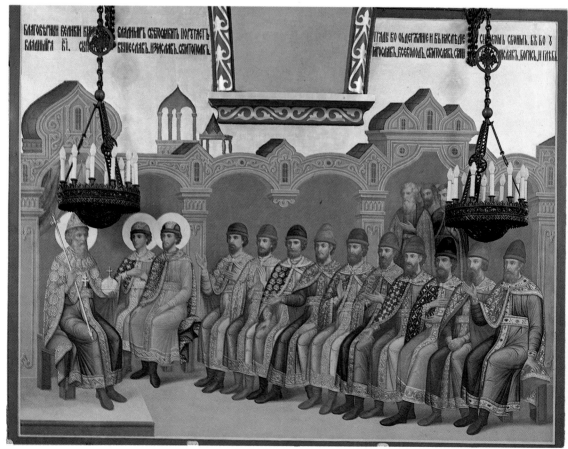

97. *The Faceted Palace.*
Grand Prince Vladimir and His Sons.
Painting on the east wall. Detail

It is not by chance that the picture
of Kievan Prince Vladimir with his
twelve sons takes pride of place in
the mural on the east wall of the
Faceted Palace. Vladimir was the
first Russian prince to convert to
Christianity, baptizing all his sons
and all the citizens of Kiev. The
year 988, when the new religion
was officially adopted, is an important date in the history of Old
Russia. After his death, Prince Vladimir was canonized, along with Boris
and Gleb, two of his sons who died
a martyr's death in a fratricidal
struggle for the throne. All three
are depicted on the fresco with
golden halos around their heads.

98. *The Faceted Palace.*
Tsar Fiodor Seated on His Throne.
Painting on the south wall. Detail

99. *The Faceted Palace. West wall*
and window of the secret room

This composition representing Tsar
Fiodor on his throne, embodies all
the most characteristic features of
the murals in the Faceted Palace. It
is notable for its vivid imagery and
extreme decorativeness of style. The
painters paid much attention to various coloristic details of old Russian dress and jewellery and also to
patterns on cloth. In this respect,
the Palekh artists definitely strove
to emulate the seventeenth-century
Russian decorative manner of
painting.

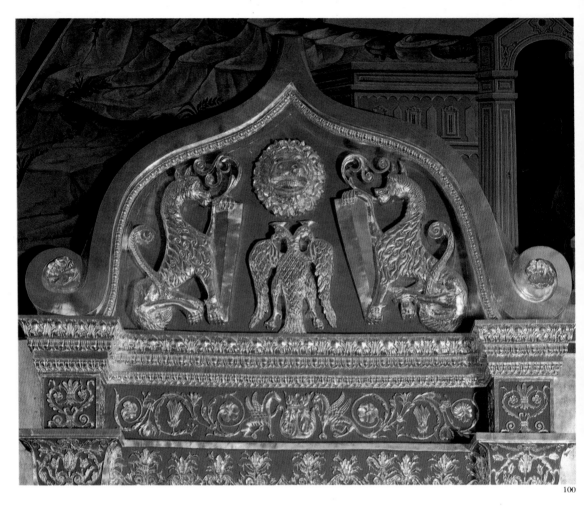

100. *The Faceted Palace.*
Inner portal. Detail

101. *The Faceted Palace.*
Carving on the central pier

The single central pier of the palace
is embellished by a bas-relief with
dolphins. This carved decor has had
a chequered history: at one time it
was thought to have been irrevo-
cably lost. The reliefs were
originally cut off in the eighteenth
century. The pier was obscured on
each side, right up to the cornice,
by *postavets*-container shelves.
In 1881–82, when the murals in the
palace were being repainted, the
pier was decorated with figures of
dolphins. Executed on detachable
wooden panels, it echoed
the motif of the ancient white

limestone carvings. In the course of
restoration work during the 1960s,
the panels were removed, uncovering clear traces of the original
stone relief. The pier was then re-
carved to the old design. On
each of the central facets there
are depictions of dolphins, with
their heads down, facing each other
as though they were diving. They
are all arranged symmetrically
around the sides of a candelabrum
and bordered by square depressions
in which figures of animals and
birds alternate. Two narrow bands
of delicate plant ornament in the
Renaissance style adorn the lower
part of the pier. The square depressions with their somewhat naive decorative representations of animals
were obviously added to the pier
later than the main carvings. All

the reliefs were gilded in 1968, and
effectively offset the red terracotta
background of the pier, which was
repainted at the same time.

102. *The Tsarina's Golden Chamber. Portal*

Thanks to the efforts of Soviet experts, the portal of the Tsarina's Golden Chamber has been restored to its original splendour. This portal is interesting in that it illustrates how Russian craftsmen adapted Western European architectural forms. The stone carving on the fully profiled cornice and the frame of the doorway is quintessentially Russian. Though its ornament is rich in diverse elements linked by complex interwoven arabesques, it is nevertheless easy to "decipher". One noteworthy fact is that the ornamental carvings on the portal of the chamber have a great deal in common with the decorative patterns on the precious plate and icon mountings made by Kremlin metalsmiths at the end of the sixteenth century. Many of these items are now on show in the Armoury.

103. *The Tsarina's Golden Chamber. Northwestern section*

With its abundant murals, fancifully shaped windows, seven niches, and unusual cross arches, the interior of the Tsarina's Golden Chamber is typical of those in old Russian palaces. On the walls, priceless fragments of ancient frescoes are visible beneath the later layers of paint. The masterfully executed compositions seem at one with the surrounding architecture, and the diverse ornament is a pleasure to behold. The chamber doors lend the interior great charm and historical authenticity. They are covered with red fabric and decorated with a design of gilded nail-heads and openwork plaques copied from extant samples of the seventeenth century. The doors were refurbished in 1979 by M. Kostikov under the supervision of N. Pomerantsev, Merited Artist of the Russian Federation.

104. *The Tsarina's Golden Chamber. Painting on the south and west walls*

The frescoes in the Tsarina's Golden Chamber depict themes from the history of the Christian Church which are sometimes based on actual events and facts. Scenes of conflict and struggle often appear in these multifigure compositions.
The frescoes on the west and south walls are devoted to episodes from the history of iconoclasm in eighth- and ninth-century Byzantium.

One scene, rendered in interesting detail, shows the Empress Theodora beseeching God to forgive her husband, Emperor Theophilus (r. 829–842), an early supporter of the iconoclasts. After his death Theodora revived icon-worship in Byzantium, for which she was later canonized. The large figure of St Theodora, wearing a crown and with a halo round her head, is placed in the bottom part of the vault. She is portrayed wearing a typical seventeenth-century Russian gown and headdress.

105. *The Tsarina's Golden Chamber. Windows and niches*

106. *The Tsarina's Golden Chamber*. Princess Olga's Journey to Constantinople. *Painting on the east wall. Detail*

The east wall of the Tsarina's Golden Chamber is embellished by frescoes devoted to Olga, a princess of Old Russia. The first picture in the cycle, a portrayal of Princess Olga setting out to be baptized at Tsargrad (Constantinople), delights the viewer with its spontaneity and well-observed details. It shows a small, cosy carriage bowling along, drawn by a pair of horses, one of which is being driven by a coachman. Olga and her servant are sitting on wooden seats under the arch of the carriage cover. The princess is wearing a richly embroidered robe and a cloak; her flowing white coif is surmounted by a crown of indented design. Outriders can be seen behind the carriage. The landscape background beyond includes the walls and fortress towers.

107. *The Tsarina's Golden Chamber*. Queen Dinara. *Painting on the north wall. Detail*

The composition on the north wall (behind and to the right of the arch) relates the tale of Queen Dinara, who fought against the Persians (Dinara is identified with the Georgian Queen Tamar). The murals stress Dinara's military prowess: she is depicted wearing armour, mounted on a galloping white horse, a crown of indented design on her head and a pale blue cloak billowing out behind her. The soft highlights and the golden blaze of the helmets and armour give an idea of what the murals originally looked like.

108

108. *The Tsarina's Golden
Chamber. Painting on the north
wall. Detail*

THE PALACE CHURCHES OF THE 14th TO 17th CENTURIES

The Great Kremlin Palace incorporated the series of churches belonging to the tsar's residence: the Church of the Raising of Lazarus, the Church of the Nativity of the Virgin, the Church of Our Saviour behind the Golden Gate (Verkhospassky), the Church of the Resurrection Glorified, the Church of the Crucifixion, and St Catherine's Church. In the past, the Church of the Redeemer in the Wood, the Church of the Deposition of the Robe and the Cathedral of the Annunciation were also considered to be palace churches. The first of these, however, was torn down at the beginning of the 1930s, and the other two have functioned as museums since 1918. The churches which now form part of the palace are outstanding examples of fourteenth- to seventeenth-century Russian architecture. They house a priceless collection of Russian representational and applied art amassed over many centuries.

109. *The Church of the Raising of Lazarus. Central section*

110. *The Church of the Raising of Lazarus. Portal*

111. *The Church of the Raising of Lazarus. Altar*

The Church of the Raising of Lazarus is a gem of fourteenth- to seventeenth-century Russian architecture. The monumental forms of the building, the massive columns supporting the vaults, the plastic expressiveness of the west portal, the wall niches, and the doorways are all characteristic features of white limestone architecture in Moscow at the end of the fourteenth century. Although during the course of later reconstructions and alterations the original height of the vault was lowered by one-third, the southeast corner and two apses relaid in brick, the north entrance with its ancient murals torn down, and the south portal redesigned (in imitation of seventeenth-century structures), the church has not lost its grandeur. It was originally known as the Church of the Nativity of the Virgin, because it was dedicated to the victory of Russian forces over the Tatar horde of Khan Mamai at the Battle of Kulikovo. This famous event took place on September 8, 1380, a date celebrated in the religious calendar as the day of Virgin Mary's birth; the victory was therefore considered to be beneath her protection. The construction was undertaken by order of Princess Eudoxia, the widow of Dmitry Donskoi, the Russian commander. According to the annals, the church was erected "near the bedchambers", i.e. close to the living quarters, on the site where a small wooden Church of the Raising of Lazarus had earlier stood. The chronicler held the new church in high esteem, calling it "very wonderful". He informs us that the Grand Princess embellished it with gold and silver vessels, and also that it was painted with frescoes in 1395 by Theophanes the Greek, Semion Chorny, and their pupils.

During the fifteenth century, the church was damaged several times. In 1405 the part of the side-chapel near the altar was struck by lightning; in 1445 the cross on the roof was knocked down in a storm; in 1454 it was again struck by lightning; and in 1479 the roof fell in. In 1514 Alevisio Novi built a new vault to replace the ruined one; the new structure was not of white limestone but of brick. On top of it the architect erected a five-domed church which retained the name of the Church of the Nativity of the Virgin; the one remaining below was renamed the Chapel of the Raising of Lazarus. Walled up and forgotten, it was not rediscovered until the nineteenth century, when the Great Kremlin Palace was being built. The white limestone floor was then relaid, and the walls and columns replastered and painted with fresh murals. From 1923 to 1928,

112

only a few years before it was torn down and replaced by a single-dome church.

The interior and exterior of the Church of the Nativity of the Virgin took on their present appearance in the nineteenth century, when the new Great Kremlin Palace was erected and the ancient structures renovated. In the 1840s the walls of the church and refectory were decorated with paintings from drawings by Solntsev. The tiers of icons in the tall iconostasis are surrounded by a gilded metal mounting with a chased pattern executed in the seventeenth-century style. The iconostasis incorporates many works of high artistic merit, a number of which can be attributed to seventeenth-century royal icon-painters. New icons, many with especially opulent mountings, are known to have been added to the iconostasis in the eighteenth century. The mountings were later taken away and the icons were included in the general framework of the iconostasis.

The most interesting items of applied art preserved in the church are those dating from the seventeenth century: the old, traditionally tiled stove in the refectory, and the lighting fixtures — large, chased candlesticks of Baroque form and a many-tiered chandelier. The central shaft of the chandelier consists of separate pieces threaded together and finishes at the base in a large ornamental sphere. The S-shaped arms branching off from the shaft support holders embellished with many cast and forged scrolls, which form a beautiful interwoven openwork pattern between the tiers of the chandelier.

the Soviet architects and scholars D. Sukhov and N. Pomerantsev made a thorough study of the ancient white limestone church and partially reconstructed it.

A final restoration of the interior was carried out between 1949 and 1952 on the basis of their work: the walls and vaults were cleaned of nineteenth-century murals, exposing the ancient limestone masonry.

112. *The Church of the Nativity of the Virgin. Holy Gates*

113. *The Church of the Nativity of the Virgin. Iconostasis*

Built by Alevisio Novi in 1514, the Church of the Nativity of the Virgin has undergone several reconstructions, the largest of which took place in 1681–85. At this time, a refectory was built, the five domes were taken down, and the church and refectory vaults were used as the foundation for a new church, the Cathedral of the Descent of the Holy Spirit. The cathedral lasted

114, 115, *The Cathedral of Our Saviour (Verkhospassky).*
Iconostasis

The stately exterior of the Cathedral of Our Saviour was echoed by the rows of icons in the iconostases of the church and its side-chapels. The icons were executed by the best royal artists in the Armoury workshops, which in the second half of the seventeenth century played the role of the main artistic centre in Russia. Drawing on the creative experience of Western European, Oriental, Ukrainian, and Byelo-russian painters, the artists of the Armoury worked out a new style which came to typify the Kremlin school of icon-painters. One of its most talented representatives was Fiodor Zubov, who came from a family of icon-painters in Veliky Ustiug. He was considered one of the leading masters of the Armoury and even received a yearly salary from the tsar. Although there was a distinction between icon-painters and painters at that time, in practice both groups of artists did a wide variety of work: they painted murals and ceilings in cathedrals and palace chambers, and decorated banners, camp tents, games and toys, furniture, carriages, and harness. In addition to all this, they painted icons, portraits and miniatures. Zubov often collaborated with Simon Ushakov on various orders for the royal court. Two of the icons in the lower tier of the iconostasis are ascribed to Zubov: *Longinus the Centurion* and *Theodore Stratelates.* Executed in 1680, they are stylistically close to the work of Simon Ushakov. Zubov, like Ushakov, tended towards realism and attempted to give the saints tangible

116. *The Cathedral of Our Saviour (Verkhospassky). The icon of* **Longinus the Centurion** *by Fiodor Zubov*

Tradition holds that Longinus was the Roman centurion who was in charge of the men guarding the Cross with Christ crucified on it at Golgotha.
Later, he was baptized and began preaching the Gospel himself. He died a martyr's death for his beliefs, and was later canonized. Longinus is portrayed in full panoply, with a cloak thrown over decorated armour. A veil is wrapped round his head and falls on to his shoulders. His countenance, full of mournful concentration, is directed towards the Cross he is holding in front of himself.

human features, while preserving the traditional iconographic scheme.
Both icons betray Zubov's impeccable skill as a decorator.
Other icons in the lower tier, including the *Vernicle* with twenty border scenes, are the work of Zubov's contemporaries, Leonty Stepanov and Sergei Kostromitin (Rozhkov). The chased silver mounting on the middle part of the iconostasis was made in 1788 and is one of the few extant monumental examples of eighteenth-century Russian toreutics. The large subject compositions on

the mounting, *The Synaxis of the Virgin, The Trinity* and *The Annunciation,* reveal the engraver's extraordinary ability to construct multifigure scenes, convey space, and depict people and landscapes. His freely executed reliefs attain great plastic expressiveness.
At the same time the ornamental elements of the silver panels are carefully and tastefully worked. The elaborateness of the compositions, the abundance of fragmentary swirling drapes, the ornamental pattern of the background, and the

pronounced light and shade effects, all indicate that the engraver was an adherent of the Baroque style. The mounting must have been crafted by one of the prominent Moscow silversmiths of the late eighteenth century.

117. *The Cathedral of Our Saviour (Verkhospassky). The icon of* Theodore Stratelates by *Fiodor Zubov*

Theodore Stratelates lived at the beginning of the fourth century. He was an army commander (*stratelates* in Greek) in the town of Hiraklion on the southern shore of the Pontus Euxinus, and had a reputation as a brave warrior and wise man. By the order of Roman Emperor Licinius, Strate-lates, who preached the Gospel zealously, was put to death. He was canonized, and is known as the patron saint of warriors.

118

118. *The Church of the Resurrection Glorified. Choir*

119. *The Church of the Resurrection Glorified. Iconostasis*

After the Church of the Crucifixion, painted in soft, restrained shades, the colour scheme of the Church of the Resurrection Glorified seems strikingly exuberant. The carved, gilded and silvered iconostasis and choir feature Baroque forms. Carving of this type became widespread in Russia during the second half of the seventeenth century; its quick flourishing was largely brought about by the establishment of closer cultural links with a number of Western European countries and also Poland, the Ukraine and Byelorussia, where high relief carving in the Baroque style was extensively used to decorate both secular and ecclesiastical buildings. New carving designs came to Russia via itinerant crafstmen, and also via illustrated editions or single pages of Western European prints, which were known at the time as "foreign sheets". The carving on the iconostasis and choir in the Church of the Resurrection is executed in high relief, graduating to openwork and circular forms. Some details of the ornament were cut separately and then fastened to the surface. As well as rich and varied plant designs such as grape-vines, leaves and fruit, there are different kinds of cartouches, delineated by fanciful curved lines and accentuated by comb-shaped ornaments, spiral volutes and beads. The carved pattern of the choir is amplified by intricately profiled brackets with a design of stylized grasses.

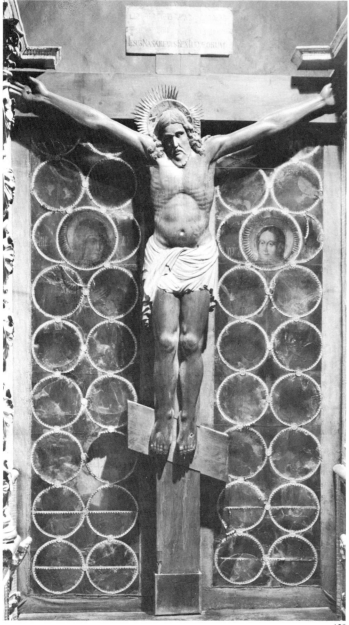

120. *The Church of the Crucifixion.*
Cypress crucifix in the Oratory

In the second half of the seventeenth century, the art of carving
reached great heights in the
workshops of the Kremlin. Skilled
craftsmen from the Armoury and
the Office of the Great Sovereign's
Palace could barely keep up with
the numerous orders for the royal
residences and churches.
The large cedar and cypress crucifix
in the chapel of the Church of the
Crucifixion was made by Russian
craftsmen in 1687. It was probably
intended for the ceremony known as
the Exaltation of the Life-giving
Cross; old records indicate that it
was "made in the likeness of and
the same size as the Life-giving
Cross".
The authors of this sculptural image
must have belonged to the circle of
the seventeenth-century carvers, the
venerable Hyppolite and Arsenius
and craftsman Klim Mikhailov.
Behind the crucifix, there is an old
icon-case with small icons in round
mica frames.

120

121. *The Church of the Crucifixion.
Holy Gates*

The sixteenth-century Holy Gates in
the Church of the Crucifixion are a
remarkable example of decorative
applied art. They are cut of
limewood and embellished with skilful ornamental carvings which almost seem to "carpet" the entire
surface. This dense pattern, satu-
rated with stylized elements, forms a
background against which the delicate icon-cases in the shape of small
onion-domed churches stand out
sharply in higher relief. The cases
contain miniature icons with a scene
of the Annunciation and figures of
the Evangelists. The Holy Gates
have long been used as an entrance
to the galleries of the neighbouring
Church of the Resurrection.
They were formerly kept in the
Church of the Deposition of the
Robe, where they found their way
from the patriarchal village of
Troitsky-Golenishchev.

122

122. *The Church of the Crucifixion. The icon of the* Last Judgment *with appliqué work*

In the Church of the Crucifixion and the Oratory there are some unique works of seventeenth-century art, executed by Bogdan Saltanov, Ivan Bezmin and Vasily Poznansky in the "taffeta-painting" technique, which combined painted images with appliqué done in rare kinds of material. This technique was very popular in Moscow in the 1680s. Some Russian art historians think that the icon-pictures done for the Church of the Crucifixion constitute the first order completed solely by artists, without the participation of icon-painters. Among these works, *Adoration of the Cross* (known from an early eighteenth-century copy) and *The Last Judgement*, both dating from 1677–78, deserve particular attention.

THE TEREM
PALACE

The lavish, festive and picturesque appearance of the Terem Palace has delighted and impressed people over the centuries. This is amply attested by numerous accounts of both Russians and foreigners who were lucky enough to see the "exceedingly wonderful palaces". The fairy-tale magnificence of the Terem Palace is enhanced by the Golden Gate in the courtyard in front of the Golden Porch.

124

123, 124. *The Golden Gate on
the Verkhospassky Landing in front
of the Terem Palace*

125. *The Golden Porch of
the Terem Palace*

The stairs which led from the Boyar
Gathering-place to the Terem Palace were redecorated in the second
half of the seventeenth century; in
1670, the Golden Gate was added
to the gilded white stone lions on
the parapets. It barred the head of
the stairway on the Verkhospassky
Landing. The gilded and painted
gate with its original design, which
does not reappear on the other
three flights of stairs, earned these
steps the title of Golden Staircase.
An extension of the staircase,
the Golden Porch gave access to
the living quarters. It has survived
intact to this day, whereas the
staircase has undergone
alterations and now leads from the
St Vladimir Hall to its galleries and
to the Golden Gate.

The Golden Porch has an expressive
and elegant composition. Its dimensions, forms and decor accord with
its function as the main entrance to
the tsar's living quarters in the
seventeenth century. However, the
alterations made during the 1830s
affected the outward appearance of
the porch. The shining gilt which
had for centuries embellished the
roof and inner walls and which had
given the porch its name was over-
laid with oil-paintings. The small
area in front of the porch was covered with a flat roof, the floor was
laid with oak parquet, and the outer
arches were fitted with glass. Since
these changes were introduced during the construction of the Great
Kremlin Palace for Nicholas I, the
shields held by the lions on the
Golden Porch bear his monogram.

126

126. *The Golden Porch of the Terem Palace. Detail of the arch*

In the architecture of the Terem Palace wide use is made of the motif of the double arch with pendant. Particularly noteworthy are pendants of the arches in the Golden Porch. They are shaped as lion masks, holding in their jaws the apple of silence — symbol that the secrets of the tsar's house be never divulged.

127. *The Golden Porch of the Terem Palace. Portal and the entrance to the Anteroom*

128. *The Terem Palace. Anteroom*

The entrance to the Terem Palace is clearly visible through the double arch on the upper landing of the Golden Porch. The stone portal of the Anteroom, which opens on to the porch, is decorated with carvings and gilt. Up till now, only one side of the portal has been stripped down to the original gilt; the other is still covered with nineteenth-century oil-paintings. The Terem Palace is modelled in many respects on the wooden architecture of Old Russia. Its interiors

are intimate and cosy, totally different from those of the stately Faceted Palace. The rooms, rather cramped by modern standards, with low vaulted ceilings, small windows and antique furniture, reflect a tenor of life still rather shut-in and far removed from the outside world. Other aspects of this life-style are also evident, such as the striving for a picturesque interior decor.

129—131. *The Terem Palace.*
Cross, or Assembly Room

It is not difficult to imagine how
gay the grand houses of Old Russia
looked with their carved decor, how
beautifully the portals, the ribs of
the vaults and the lacy fretwork of
the oak window-sills harmonized
with the coloured tiled stoves,
the bright murals, the mica
window-panes, the variegated fabrics, and the painted and gilded
furniture. Just such a motley decor
has been preserved in the Cross, or
Assembly Room.

132, 133. *The Terem Palace. Study*

In the Study, the seventeenth-century decor has probably survived more fully than in any other of the rooms. It is recorded that in the 1660s the royal icon-painter Simon Ushakov decorated the Sovereign's Room (i.e. the Study) with gold blades of grass against a red ground. From old accounts we know that in 1666 the doors of the Study were decorated with gilt and embossed leather, patterned with beasts and plants. The murals, executed by Timofei Kiseliov in the 1830s after designs by Academician Solntsev, were undoubtedly completed according to the latter's instructions, based on a thorough study of the room. The main motifs are grasses, beasts and coats-of-arms, against a red background with gold ornamentation. During restoration in the 1970s, the ornamentation of the murals, the ribs of the vaults and the portals of the Study were regilded.
One of the genuine antiques in the room is a small carved table

made in the second half of the seventeenth century in the Baroque style. Its top is worked in oils to resemble marble, and its four carved S-shaped legs are painted bright blue, with a thick layer of gilt on their outer surface.
During the reign of Tsar Alexei Mikhailovich and especially that of his son Fiodor Alexeyevich, the Armoury craftsmen and the gilders in the workshop of the Ambassadors' Office often received orders for this kind of furniture, intended for use in the royal chambers. The orders were accompanied by instructions such as "cover the carpentry with carving" or "gild completely and paint on a design". To the right, near the wall, there is a round stove, set with gaily coloured tiles and culminating in an indented crown similar in shape to the *koruna,* a headdress worn by girls in Old Russia. The shining glazed tiles on the stove are reminiscent of the precious enamel found on *objets d'art* crafted by seventeenth-century Russian goldsmiths.
As well as the doors which link the

Study with the other rooms in the suite, there are two others, also set in carved, gilded portals. The first leads to the Pantry, a small rectangular room formerly used to prepare light snacks for serving in the Study (the Pantry still contains cupboards and a table of antique design). The second gives access to a narrow indoor spiral staircase made of stone, which connects the floors of the Terem Palace and ends on the landing in front of the Upper Teremok and Watch-tower.

134. *The Terem Palace. Carving on a window-sill in the Study*

135. *The Terem Palace. Bedchamber*

The main point of interest here is the carved wooden bed, topped by a "sky"-type canopy. Intricately decorated beds were highly prized in the seventeenth century; Tsar Alexei Mikhailovich is known to have placed orders with furniture-makers accompanied by the instructions: "make a carved wooden bed and cover all the surfaces with gilt". Although the murals in the Bedchamber contain four subject tondo compositions, they remain purely decorative in character and include freely reinterpreted motifs from sixteenth-century Italian ornament. The plant designs on the walls and ceiling match the wood-carvings on the bed in the centre and the silk upholstery fabric on the chairs and benches set along the walls.

136. *The Terem Palace. Oratory*

Though the very function of the Oratory presupposes a wider use of religious representations, its interior decor is in fact based on ornamental designs. Grasses — luxuriant, whimsical, fairy-tale patterns of variegated stems, leaves and flowers typical of old Russian ornament — predominate in the murals. This motif is echoed by the curling vines and bunches of grapes which stand out in relief against the columns of the iconostases. The two gilded iconostases preserved in the Oratory are characteristic examples of Russian monumental decorative carving in the late seventeenth and early eighteenth centuries.

137. *The Terem Palace.*
Upper Teremok (Attic)

The fifth storey of the Terem Palace, known as the Upper Teremok,
is a large rectangular chamber with
numerous windows and two lovely
stoves with many of their antique
tiles still intact. White limestone
carving is used in exceptional abundance for the decoration of the
Teremok. On the vaults there are
carved braids which intersect, run
down to the walls and end in figured shields with fantastic creatures.
The inner and outer portals and
window-surrounds are covered with
intricate, interlacing patterns, and
the window-cornices are embellished
with figures of animals and birds.
Details from coats-of-arms and
fairy-tale motifs are widely incorporated into the ornament.

138. *The Terem Palace.*
Upper Teremok. Portal. Detail

The western entrance into the
Upper Teremok and neighbouring
Watch-tower from the landing is
framed by a carved white limestone
portal with a five-pointed arch and
a pediment. The portal is striking
for its nobly restrained forms and
lines, its simple, expressive proportions and its light, elegant ornament.

LIST OF ILLUSTRATIONS
SELECTED BIBLIOGRAPHY

ILLUSTRATIONS
IN THE TEXT

SELECTED
BIBLIOGRAPHY

П. Агеев
*Краткий указатель достопримеча-
тельностей Большого Кремлевско-
го дворца в Москве* [P. Ageyev.
*A Short Guide to the Places of In-
terest in the Great Kremlin Palace
in Moscow*], Moscow, 1865

С. П. Бартенев
*Большой Кремлевский дворец.
Указатель к его обозрению*
[S. Bartenev, *The Great Kremlin
Palace. A Guidebook*], Moscow,
1911

С. П. Бартенев
*Московский Кремль в старину и
теперь* [S. Bartenev, *The Moscow
Kremlin in Olden Times and
Today*], vol. 2, Moscow, 1916

А. Бенуа, Н. Лансере
*"Дворцовое строительство Нико-
лая I"*. Старые годы [A. Benois,
N. Lanceray, Palace Construction
in the Reign of Nicholas I", *Starye
Gody*], St Petersburg, 1913, July–
September

Л. Берзите
*Развитие национальных форм в
архитектуре Московского Кремля*
[L. Berzite, *The Development of
National Forms in the Architecture
of the Moscow Kremlin*], Riga,
1954

А. Вельтман
*Описание нового императорского
дворца в Кремле Московском*
[A. Weltman, *A Description of the
New Imperial Palace in the Moscow
Kremlin*], Moscow, 1851

Н. В. Гордеев
Большой Кремлевский дворец
[N. Gordeyev, *The Great Kremlin
Palace*], Moscow, 1957

Н. В. Гордеев
*Большой Кремлевский дворец.
Памятник русской архитектуры*

[N. Gordeyev, *The Great Kremlin
Palace, a Monument of Russian
Architecture*], Moscow, 1967

И. Е. Забелин
*Материалы для истории, археоло-
гии и статистики города Москвы*
[I. Zabelin, *Materials on the
History, Archaeology and Statistics
of the City of Moscow*], part I,
Moscow, 1884

И. Е. Забелин
*Домашний быт русского народа в
XVI и XVII столетиях* [I. Zabelin,
*The Family Life of the Russian
People in the 16th and 17th centu-
ries*], vols. 1, 2, Moscow, 1862–69

В. Н. Иванов
Московский Кремль [V. Ivanov,
The Moscow Kremlin], Moscow,
1970

Н. Д. Извеков
*"Московские кремлевские двор-
цовые церкви и служившие при
них лица в XVII веке"*, Труды
комиссии по осмотру и изучению
памятников церковной старины
г. Москвы и Московской епархии
[N. Izvekov, "The Palace Churches
of the Moscow Kremlin and the
People Who Served in Them during
the Seventeenth Century", *Transactions of the Commission for the In-
spection and Study of Monuments
of Ancient Church Architecture
in the City and See of Moscow*],
vol. 2, Moscow, 1906

История Москвы [*The History of
Moscow*], vols. 1, 2, Moscow,
1952–53

История русской архитектуры
[*The History of Russian Architecture*], Moscow, 1956

История русского искусства
[*The History of Russian Art*], vol. I,
Moscow, 1978

Е. И. Кириченко
Москва. Памятники архитектуры 1830–1910-х годов [E. Kirichenko, *Moscow. Architectural Monuments of the Period 1830–1910*], Moscow, 1977

Е. И. Кириченко
Русская архитектура 1830–1910-х годов [E. Kirichenko, *Russian Architecture of the Period 1830–1910*], Moscow, 1978

Н. Н. Коваленская
История русского искусства. Первая половина XIX века [N. Kovalenskaya, *The History of Russian Art. The First Half of the Nineteenth Century*], Moscow, 1951

Н. Левинсон, Л. Гончарова
Русская художественная бронза [N. Levinson, L. Goncharova, *Russian Bronzework*], Moscow, 1958

Г. А. Маркова
Большой Кремлевский дворец [G. Markova, *The Great Kremlin Palace*], Moscow, 1975

G. Markowa
Der Kreml, Leipzig, 1975

Moskauer Kreml. Architektur und Malerei, Prag, 1965

Н. Е. Мнева
Искусство Московской Руси. Вторая половина XV–XVII в. [N. Mneva, *The Art of Muscovy from the Second Half of the Fifteenth to the Seventeenth Century*], Moscow, 1965

Московский Кремль [*The Moscow Kremlin*], Moscow, 1965

A. Nasibova
The Faceted Chamber in the Moscow Kremlin, Leningrad, 1978

Ю. М. Овсянников
Солнечные плитки. Рассказы об изразцах [Yu. Ovsiannikov, "Gleam-ing Tiles". Short Stories about Tiles], Moscow, 1967

А. А. Потапов
"Очерк древней русской гражданской архитектуры", *Труды императорского археологического общества* [A. Potapov, "A Study of Old Russian Civil Architecture", *Transactions of the Imperial Archaeological Society*], vol. 19, 2nd ed., Moscow, 1901

Л. Писарская, И. Родимцева
Московский Кремль [L. Pisarskaya, I. Rodimtseva, *The Moscow Kremlin*], Moscow, 1972

По Кремлю. Путеводитель [*Through the Kremlin. A Guidebook*], Moscow, 1960

Русское декоративное искусство [*Russian Decorative Art*], vols. 1–3, Moscow, 1962–65

Н. П. Собко
"Ф. Г. Солнцев и его художественно-археологическая деятельность", *Вестник изящных искусств* [N. Sobko, "F. Solntsev and His Artistic and Archaeological Activity", *Vestnik Iziashchnykh Iskusstv*], vol. 3, Moscow, 1883

Т. М. Соколова
Художественная мебель [T. Sokolova, *Decorative Furniture*], Leningrad, 1967

К. А. Соловьев
Русский художественный паркет [K. Solovyov, *Russian Decorative Parquetry*], Moscow, 1963

Н. Я. Тихомиров, В. Н. Иванов
Московский Кремль. История архитектуры [N. Tikhomirov, V. Ivanov, *The History of the Architecture of the Moscow Kremlin*], Moscow, 1967

А. Успенский
Царские иконописцы и живописцы XVII века [A. Uspensky, *The Royal Icon-Painters and Artists of the Seventeenth Century*], Moscow, 1913

Художественные памятники Московского Кремля [*Artistic Monuments of the Moscow Kremlin*], Moscow, 1966

С. Шальнов
В. И. Ленин в Большом Кремлевском дворце [S. Shalnov, *Lenin in the Great Kremlin Palace*], Moscow, 1963

БОЛЬШОЙ
КРЕМЛЕВСКИЙ
ДВОРЕЦ

Альбом (на английском языке)
Издание третье

Издательство „Аврора". Ленинград. 1990
Изд. № 2256. (9-00)
Printed and bound in Yugoslavia